A LITTLE GIANT® BOOK

TRICKS & PRANKS

E. Richard Churchill

STERLING

New York / London

www.sterlingpublishing.com/kids

Library of Congress Cataloging-in-Publication Data Available

Lot#: 10 9 8 7 6

09/11

Published by Sterling Publishing Co., Inc.
387 Park Avenue South, New York, NY 10016
© 2005 by Sterling Publishing Co., Inc.
Material in this book originally published in *Sneaky Tricks to Fool Your Friends*, ©
1986 by E. Richard Churchill; *More Tricks to Fool Your Friends*, by E. Richard
Churchill. © 1985 by Sterling Publishing Co., Inc.
Distributed in Canada by Sterling Publishing
c/o Canadian Manda Group, 165 Dufferin Street
Toronto, Ontario, Canada M6K 3H6
Distributed in the United Kingdom by GMC Distribution Services,
Castle Place, 166 High Street, Lewes, East Sussex, England BN7 1XU
Distributed in Australia by Capricorn Link (Australia) Pty. Ltd.
P.O. Box 704, Windsor, NSW 2756, Australia

Sterling ISBN-13: 978-1-4027-4977-3
ISBN-10: 1-4027-4977-5

For information about custom editions, special sales, premium and
corporate purchases, please contact Sterling Special Sales
Department at 800-805-5489 or specialsales@sterlingpub.com.

CONTENTS

MISSION IMPOSSIBLE—MAYBE

PUZZLING NUMBERS, SNEAKY SHAPES

CONS WITH CARDS AND DICE

BEFORE YOU BEGIN

People have been playing tricks on friends and family for thousands of years—in many places it's almost a national sport. Why? Because it's not only fun for the trickster, it's also fun for the person who falls for the prank. The great thing is that people actually *like* being tricked. They enjoy the surprise and trying to figure out just how they were hoaxed.

The 136 tricks, stunts, and puzzles in this book are intended to give exactly that kind of double-your-fun enjoyment. Some are stunts for you to try first. Then dare others to do what you already know how to do.

Many of the pranks require some sort of physical action. Your victim may be asked to do something as simple as dropping a card or standing next to a wall. The trick is that though they seem too simple even to bother with, they simply can't be done. Others *appear* hopeless but they turn out to be easy once you've learned how to do them. (Don't worry, you'll be told if a problem truly is impossible!) Either way, you're the winner!

Keep in mind, these are not "magic tricks." You certainly could use some of them in a magic act but if you like but these are things anyone can learn to do anywhere—to amaze a whole audience or just one friend. None of these will hurt the victim of the trick and any items you need to make a stunt work can usually be found around the house or classroom, like a coin, glass or piece of paper.

Best of all, you won't need to practice any of these tricks more than a few times to make them work. Just be sure to read each trick over first to see how it's done; in some cases the solution is placed upside-down at the bottom of the page. Figure out the stunt *before* trying it on your friends and other victims and you'll be surprised how many times you can trip up even your sharpest friends.

Now, this is probably a good time for a word of advice. An old saying goes, "Don't go to the well too often." For the trickster, that saying translates to, "Don't try the same trick on the same person too often." Even the best card trick will eventually give itself away if you keep repeating it with the same victim. Do any trick, such as "The Tattletale Chosen Card," only a few times, then move on to others. And look for this illustration as you read the book. It's a reminder not to repeat that particular prank too many times.

So now you know the best trick tip of all: Don't give anyone too many opportunities to figure out how your stunt works—not if you want to be the trickiest person around!

FUNNY MONEY

Money Talks

All you need for some of the best tricks are loose change, a little practice, and quick hands. "Money Talks" is just that sort of trick.

Begin with a dollar bill. Hold it out in front of you with the face toward your audience. Make sure the top of the head is up.

Begin by folding the top half of the bill

forward and down so the face is inside the fold. The bill is now folded in half horizontally.

Now fold it in half vertically, bringing the end in your right hand over to the left.

Once again, fold the bill in half, bringing the end in your right hand over to the left.

Next, unfold the back half of the bill from your left hand toward your right. (You are unfolding two layers now.)

Then unfold the front half of the bill from your right to your left. This leaves just one fold along the top.

Finally, unfold the front of the bill upward. You now have the back of the bill toward you. Your audience sees the face of the bill exactly as it was at the beginning.

Let your victims take a quick look at the face on the bill. Then begin refolding the bill just as you did before. Repeat the first four steps: Fold the top down; fold the right side over; once again fold the right side over; unfold two layers from left to right.

Now comes the trick. The first time you unfolded the front half of the bill from right to left. This time unfold the *back* half of the bill from right to left.

When you do the last step and unfold the bill upward, something has happened. The face on the bill is now upside down.

Work on this alone until the six steps are easy for you. Practice doing the fifth step quickly and smoothly. Now you can make the head come out right side up or upside down, whichever you wish.

Since you do the folds quickly and because the change at step five is so difficult to spot, you can do this trick again and again without having people catch on.

As with many good tricks, this one is so simple it fools almost everyone!

The Tricky Dime

If you don't mind what others say when they realize they've been duped, try this one.

Place two pennies and a dime in a row, like this: penny; dime; penny.

Then say: "Without touching the dime I can shift it to the right of both pennies."

Just to keep your victim from really thinking about how this might be done, quickly add such comments as these: "I won't hit the table. I won't tip the table. I won't push the dime with a straw or a pencil or anything like that. I won't even blow on the dime."

The trick is really sneaky. It is also so simple, you can expect cries of "Cheater!" If you're going to be a real trickster, however, you'll just have to get used to the fact that people are jealous of your skills.

You said you wouldn't touch the dime but would shift it to the right of both pennies. Move the right-hand penny from where it is to the left of the other penny. Now look at the arrangement. The dime is to the right of both pennies.

Aren't you the tricky one?

Changed—But the Same

Set out five coins in the arrangement shown here. Or make up a new arrangement you like better.

"Here's the trick," you tell your friend—and stooge. "I want you to take away two coins from this group. Then I want you to add three coins so that they look just the way they do now."

"This is really tricky," you may want to add.

It does not take most people long to realize that you have asked the impossible. Some clever person may end up putting one coin on top of another. If that happens, all you have to do is to pretend to sight along the top of the desk.

"Nope," you can say. "It doesn't look the same from here."

When you're ready to prove the impossible is possible, remind your victim that you said it was really tricky.

Move any two coins to a new place on the table. That's the first part of the trick. Then add the remaining three coins to the two you just moved. You have completed the second part of the trick.

Don't pay any attention to those who say you tricked them. They are just jealous of your amazing skill!

Move One Coin

Some good tricks are simple. When a trick looks impossible and then turns out to be quite easy, it becomes a great trick. This is just that kind.

Place four coins on the table in an L shape, as shown here.

Then say something like this: "By moving only one of these coins to a new position I can make two rows of three coins in each row."

1   2   3

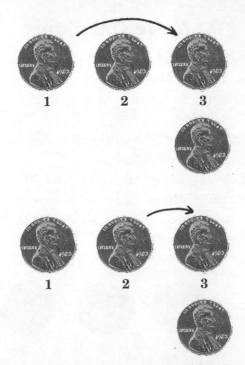

Obviously, this seems impossible. As it is now there is one row of three coins and one of two, making five altogether. It doesn't look as if anybody could make two rows of three coins each by moving only one coin. Wouldn't that come to six coins total?

Let your victim think this one over and even experiment by moving coins from one place to another, until convinced there is no way in the world to do this trick. You are ready to make your move.

Just pick up coin 1 and place it on top of coin 3. Now there are three coins in each of the two rows. For variety, you may wish to put coin 2 on top of coin 3 instead. The result is the same.

Coins on the Rim

Balance two coins on the rim of a glass as shown on the following page.

Set your victim up by saying, "I can take both those coins from the rim of the glass *at the same time*. I will touch the coins with

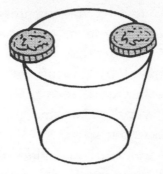

only one finger and my thumb. I won't tip the glass. I won't drop the coins. I will finish this trick holding the two coins together between my thumb and finger."

Most people have to try this trick themselves first. Let any and all give it a shot. The chances are no one will be able to figure out how you are going to do what you say.

Don't allow the glass to be moved. Make sure everyone understands the two coins must be removed from the rim at the same time.

When your victims admit this seems impossible, the spotlight is on you.

Hold the glass firmly with one hand so that it doesn't go scooting across the table while everyone has a good laugh at your expense.

Place the thumb of your other hand on one coin. Then put a finger from that same hand on the second coin. Snap both coins down from the rim onto the outside edge of the glass. Hold firmly pressed to the side of the glass so that they don't slip away.

Pull your thumb and finger together toward the front of the glass. The coins will meet and overlap. Snap the coins together between your thumb and finger and take them away from the glass. Accept any congratulations your victims may offer.

Practice this tricky trick before trying it in public. It's not hard to do, but you have to do it just as you described it to win the bet.

The Dollar Is Still Strong

A favorite way for many pranksters to introduce a trick is to pretend they don't know what they're talking about. That may be just the way to get this puzzling trick started. You'll need a dollar bill and a pencil—and you'll need to stage it near a table. It's best with more than one person in your audience.

Hold up a dollar bill and pretend to study it carefully. You may even give it a few tugs as though you're trying to see how strong the paper is.

"I read that the dollar isn't as strong as it used to be," you might say. Give the dollar in your hand another little pull. "I don't understand that. This one seems as strong as ever."

You'll probably get a big laugh. At this point, someone will explain to you that a strong dollar or a weak dollar refers to buying power. Listen carefully, but shake your head.

"This dollar [*and here you hold up the bill in your hand*] seems strong enough to me. In fact, I'll just prove it is strong."

Hold up a long pencil that you just "happen" to have handy. Ask the person who tried to explain strong and weak money to help you.

"Please hold one end of this pencil firmly against the top of this desk. I'll show you how strong this dollar bill is right now."

Place the pencil so that most of it sticks

out over the edge of the desk or table. Have your helper push down hard on the other end of the pencil, the end on the table. Position the audience so they watch from across the table.

Raise the dollar bill over your head as you hold it between your thumb and the rest of your fingers. Then, with one fast motion, bring that hand down hard. To everyone's surprise (except yours), the pencil breaks!

"See, I told you this dollar was strong." It is your turn to look pleased and even smile a little.

When the onlookers want to try this themselves you might suggest, "Let's use a different dollar bill. We already know this one is a strong dollar."

Unless others know the trick, no matter what bills they use the pencil won't break. Someone will eventually demand to try your bill.

When that happens, just shrug and lend them your dollar bill. Of course, this bill won't break the pencil either.

Now you can look puzzled and ask, "Do you suppose my strong dollar got weak?" Pick it up and sure enough, you can still break the pencil with it.

"Nope. My dollar is still strong."

How long you want to insist your dollar is strong is up to you. You can use other dollar bills and they will suddenly become "strong" in your hands.

When you run short of pencils to break, you may want to explain the trick. Or you may suddenly find your dollar is "weak" and no longer breaks pencils. It's up to you.

The trick is so simple it's hard to discover. It depends on the quick swing you make as you bring the dollar down toward the pencil.

Of course, the dollar bill won't break the pencil—but your index finger will! As your hand sweeps down, you extend your index finger, but your audience on the other side of the table doesn't see it because your finger is hidden by the dollar bill. Your finger hits the pencil and snaps it off. It's easy when you know how.

It Must Be Magic

Here is a stunt that you will enjoy doing over and over because it's so hard to figure out even when you're watching closely. Begin by folding a dollar bill in thirds, into the shape of an S, as shown below.

Hook the short, single side of one paper clip over two thicknesses of the dollar bill where they meet, as seen in the drawing. Then hook the short side of a second paper clip over the other spot where two thicknesses of the bill overlap.

While your victim watches you fold the bill, set up your bet. You casually can say something like, "I bet I can hook these two paper clips together without touching them. I'll just pull the bill away from them and they'll be hooked, due to my amazing magic powers."

Who can resist a bet like that? Once you've gotten your victim hooked, grasp each end of the bill firmly. Then, with a quick snap, tug the two ends of the bill in opposite directions. The bill will straighten out but something else happens at the same time. The two paper clips fly off the bill. And guess what? They are hooked together! You'll want to try it again to test your magic...and your eyesight.

Use Your Head

Begin by setting up six coins in a row with the first three resting heads up. The following three coins are tails up.

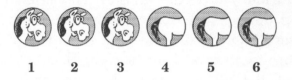

1   2   3   4   5   6

Here is the challenge. You must move the coins around so that every other coin is heads up, so the coins will alternate heads, tails, heads, tails, heads, tails.

When making changes, you must turn over two coins each time. The coins you turn over have to be side-by-side. Each move, then, means turning over any two coins that are next to each other.

You can solve the problem in only three moves. Try it yourself before testing friends.

After working it out, check to see if your solution matches this system: Turn over coins 3 and 4. Then turn over 4 and 5. Finally turn over 2 and 3.

When sure of your moves, pose this problem to others, and see how long it takes them to solve it. Some will try it a few times and tell you it is impossible. At that point you can say, "I bet I can do it." Then prove that you can.

One, Two, Three, Four

To get the attention of the people you want to confuse with this prank, begin by putting a cup on a table and slowly dropping four pennies into it. After dropping those pennies one at a time into the cup, you're bound to have the interest and attention of all.

Pour the four pennies from the cup into your hand and make your bet: "I bet I can drop these four pennies one at a time into that cup. Then I bet I can pick them up again, one at a time, and when I've picked up all four I'll still have one penny in the cup."

That sounds so impossible, someone will take you up on it.

Slowly drop the pennies into the cup, one at a time.

Then take one penny from the cup. Say, "As you can see, I've picked up one penny."

Take the second penny, narrating your action for the group. Do the same for the third penny. Then pick up the cup with the fourth penny still inside.

"See," you tell the group, "I just picked up the fourth and final penny, and it's still in the cup."

You probably won't receive great applause, but you've just won your bet.

Upsy Daisy

Arrange ten coins so they form a triangle shape. (Or make ten circles on a piece of paper.)

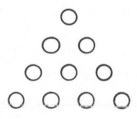

Now for the dare. Move three of the coins and only three. (Or, erase three circles and draw them in a new place.) After having moved the three coins you will have turned the pattern upside down so that it looks like this.

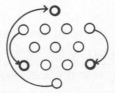

It is not all that difficult but neither is it terribly easy. If you get totally stuck or just want to check your answer, the solution is upside down.

When you have mastered this reversal it is time to challenge a friend.

Turn the page upside down for the answer.

Move the three coins to the new positions as shown by the arrows.

That's Certainly Odd!

People like to think they are too smart to be taken in by a trick. The odds are, though, that you'll be able to trick some people with any trick in this book. This one should fool quite a few.

Place ten coins beside three cups and say, "I bet I can arrange these coins so that each cup contains coins and each cup contains an *odd* number of coins."

If your dupes seem unimpressed, you can add fuel to the fire by going on to say, "I bet you can't do it."

After you've roped one in, it shouldn't take long before your victim is ready to throw in the towel. By that time, it looks like an impossible stunt. That's the point at which you are ready to win the second half of your bet.

Study the problem. Remember there is a sneaky trick to the answer. Can you see the trick and solve the problem?

Give up? The answer is easy after all. Put three coins in the first cup and three in the second. Then place four coins in the third cup and set the second cup *inside* the third cup. That third cup can now be said to contain seven coins (4 + 3) and seven is an odd number.

From One Side to the Other

Warning! Think ahead. Plan your moves. Don't fall into a trap.

With those words to guide you, this stunt should not prove impossible. Hard, yes, but never impossible. Try it first yourself to see.

You need six coins. Pennies are fine unless you are well-off and can afford dimes. On a piece of paper, draw the diagram shown at the top of page 43.

Place three coins heads up in spaces 1, 2, and 3. Leave space 4 vacant. Place the other three coins tails up in spaces 5, 6, and 7.

The object of the contest is to move the heads into spaces 5, 6, and 7, and the tails to spaces 1, 2, and 3.

There are some rules. Heads-up coins may move only to the right. Tails-up coins move only toward the left. No coin may be moved backward. A coin may move into a vacant space, but only when the vacant space is next to it. A coin may jump over a coin of a different kind to land in an empty space. (A heads-up may jump a tails-up but a tails-up may *not* jump a tails-up.)

Work on this puzzle until you can complete it in fifteen moves—turn the page upside down for the answer. Then go looking for opponents. You might say to them, "I bet I can do this puzzle in fewer moves than you can." (If you want to be on the safe side you might say, "I bet you can't complete this puzzle in fewer moves than I can.") Just be sure you can do it in fifteen moves before making your challenge, of course.

Turn the page upside down for the answer.

1.	T	T	T	H	O	H	H
2.	T	T	O	H	T	H	H
3.	T	O	T	H	T	H	H
4.	T	H	T	O	T	H	H
5.	T	H	T	H	T	O	H
6.	T	H	T	H	T	H	O
7.	T	H	T	H	O	H	T
8.	T	H	O	H	T	H	T
9.	O	H	T	H	T	H	T
10.	H	O	T	H	T	H	T
11.	H	H	T	O	T	H	T
12.	H	H	T	H	T	O	T
13.	H	H	T	H	O	T	T
14.	H	H	O	H	T	T	T
15.	H	H	H	O	T	T	T

Starting position: H H H O T T T T (0 = space)

What a Strange Arrangement

Place four dimes and four pennies on a table. Challenge your opponent using these words: "I bet I can arrange these eight coins so that I have *two rows* in which there are just two pennies in each row. There will also be *six rows* which each contain only two dimes. Oh, yes. There also will be *four rows* which have two pennies and a dime in each row."

Of course you can do it. At least, you can do it after you've worked at it for a while and then checked your answer with the upside-down answer on page 46.

You might also dare your opponent to do the job himself or herself before you show off *your* ability.

This arrangement really isn't all that difficult to see through. Just keep in mind that a row is usually defined as a straight line—and that straight lines may run in a great many directions!

Turn the page upside down for the answer.

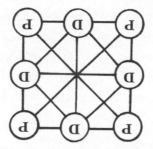

Here is the correct setup.

I Doubt That

This quick little stumper will succeed more often than you'd think, though some people will see through the trick and make a loser out of *you*.

Without showing your challenger what coins you have, put two coins in your hand. Shake them around a bit. Then, with your fist closed around the pair of coins, show your hand to your opponent.

"I've got two coins in my hand," you say. "Together they total fifteen cents. One of the coins is not a dime. I bet you can't tell me what two coins I have in my hand."

If a person doesn't see through this trick at once, it becomes almost impossible to figure out.

Can you see how it works?

If you didn't, you'll want to groan when you know the answer: The hands holds a dime and a nickel. You said one of the coins was not a dime. One wasn't. It was a nickel. The other was a dime.

You've Got to Be Kidding

Tricksters often boast that there's a sucker born every minute. To make this stunt work you have to find just one.

Have the person you've selected as the sucker take a coin from a pocket or purse. Tell the person to look closely at the date on the coin but not to tell you the date.

Next, instruct your victim to place the coin in the palm of your hand with the date down. This leaves you looking at the tail side of the coin.

Stare hard and long at the tail of the coin. Then look the poor victim in the eye and say, "I have special powers. Just by looking at this coin I can tell you the date. Do you want to bet I can't?"

Most people will want to know whether you are going to turn the coin over or drop it or any of a number of tricky things. You can honestly tell them you aren't. "I'm going to tell you the date and all I have to do is to continue to look at the tail side of the coin," is your answer.

When your bet is accepted you simply tell your victim the current day's date. After all, you never said you would tell the date on the coin. You only said you'd be able to tell the date.

Tricky, isn't it?

Money Slips Away

Did you ever notice how easily money gets away from you? It is almost like having a hole in your pocket. This problem may help show how easily money slips away.

Begin with a sheet of paper. It doesn't

have to be a very big sheet. Place a dime flat on the paper. Draw around the dime. Then carefully cut out the circle you just drew. You now have a piece of paper which looks something like a rectangular donut.

Now for the dare: You are going to push a *quarter* through the hole you just cut, and do it without tearing or ruining the paper. Give it some thought and try possible ways of doing this. You should be able to find the solution on your own. If not, or if you wish to check your solution, turn the next page upside down, and see how this stunt can be done.

Then you're ready to go looking for people

to accept your bet when you show them the dime-sized hole in your sheet and say, "I bet I can put a quarter through this hole without ripping the paper!"

Turn the page upside down for the answer.

Hold the quarter inside the folded paper so that it's positioned sideways to the hole. Grasp the coin through the hole using the fingers of one hand and, with your other hand, pinch together the top edges of the paper. Gently tug the paper upward while working the coin down sideways through the hole.

Fold and crease the paper in half so that it looks like this.

That's the Date

Have someone place a coin directly from a pocket to a tabletop, heads up. Without a glance at the coin, instruct that a piece of blank paper be placed over the coin.

Everything's in place to make your bet. "I bet I can tell you the date on that coin without touching the coin and without lifting or removing the paper from the coin," you might say.

It looks preposterous. Chances are someone will take that bet. You'll win, naturally.

How? Here's a hint: Heads, you win! But you need a soft lead pencil to help you along. Use the pencil to color over the paper that lies on top of the coin; don't let the paper slip. The coin's date will appear plainly on the paper you are blacking in with pencil lead. Neat trick.

Just practice this stunt several times

before trying it on others. It does take a bit of care in order to see the date clearly.

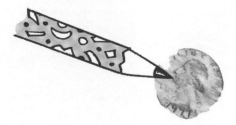

MISSION IMPOSSIBLE—MAYBE

Changing Places

Set up two quarters and a nickel on a tabletop or desk as shown here, with the nickel in the middle of the row.

Tell your patsy, "I am going to move the

25¢   5¢   25¢

right-hand quarter so that it is between the nickel and the quarter on the left."

"What's so difficult about that?" your victim will ask.

"I am not going to move the nickel. What's more I won't touch the left-hand quarter."

By now, you have everyone watching you keenly—and questioning the rules.

"Can you move the right-hand quarter?" they'll ask.

"Yes."

"Can you tip the table?"

"No. And I won't shake the table either or hit it," you'll say.

"Can you touch the nickel?"

"Yes, but I won't move it."

"You can't move the nickel and can't touch the left-hand quarter?"

"That's right," you'll boast.

"There has to be a trick to it!"

A clever victim may suggest moving the

quarter with a pencil or putting a piece of paper over it.

"That's touching it," you can tell the victim. "That quarter is only touched by the nickel and the tabletop."

You will soon be asked to perform the trick. Here it is: Put a finger down firmly on top of the nickel. Shift the right-hand quarter an inch or so to the right with your free hand.

Then quickly slide that quarter to hit hard against the side of the nickel. The nickel won't move but the quarter on the left will bounce an inch or so away from the nickel. That leaves plenty of room for you to move the right-hand quarter between the other two coins.

Without Lifting Your Pencil

Draw the square and circle shown on page 59 on a piece of paper. (Don't worry about making the square exactly square or the circle perfectly round.)

Show this drawing to your victim.

"I can draw this figure without lifting my pencil from the paper. Can you?"

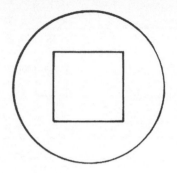

Unless your friend knows the trick, there's no way to make such a drawing without lifting the pencil from the paper.

When you're asked to show the trick, it's really quite simple.

Draw the square without lifting your pencil. When you finish, keep the point of the pencil on the paper.

Now, fold a corner of the paper over until it touches the edge of the pencil point. Slide the pencil point onto this folded paper. Continue drawing near the fold for about an

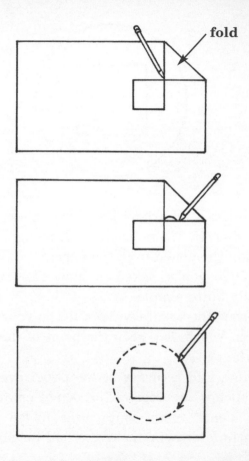

fold

inch. Then draw the pencil point back off the folded part.

The pencil point is now on the original drawing about an inch from the square you drew first. Draw the circle now.

That's all there is to making the impossible easy.

The Reversing Arrow

Draw an arrow, like the one shown below, on a piece of paper or a file card. Make it good and dark and about an inch long.

Lean the paper or card against something so that it stands up with the arrow pointing to your right. Now you can set up your victim by saying:

"See how that arrow points to my right? I can make it look like it's pointing to my left!"

Here is an important part of this trick. You said you can make it "look" like the arrow points left. You did not say you would make it point left.

"I can do this without touching the paper or moving it in any way," you say.

Obviously, this sounds impossible. So your victim will probably ask a bunch of questions to pin you down.

You will not touch the paper?

You won't move the table?

You don't have to move the paper?

You won't go around and look through the paper from the other side?

When you are ready to spring the trap all you need to do is fill a glass with water. Place the glass in front of the arrow. Move the glass forward or backward until the arrow points left when you look at it through the water in the glass.

It's as simple as that. The glass full of water becomes a lens, which reverses the arrow when it's the proper distance from the paper or card. It also makes the arrow appear longer than it really is, by the way.

Stronger than It Looks

For this trick, you need a sheet of paper about six inches wide and eight inches long. Notebook paper will work just fine.

Place two glasses on a tabletop or desk so that they are four or five inches apart.

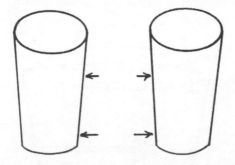

Partially fill a third glass with water and set it near the two empty glasses. Pretend to look carefully at the sheet of paper.

"You know, paper is a lot stronger than it looks."

Place the paper on top of the two glasses so that it reaches from one glass top to the other. By now you should have the attention of your victim or victims.

"In fact," you'll say (here you may hesitate a bit), "I think this paper is strong enough to hold up the glass with the water in it." You may want to point to the glass that is partially filled with water so that there is no misunderstanding.

"Yes, I'm sure of it. This piece of paper is so strong, I know it will hold the third glass between the other two."

Then the questions will begin. Stay cool and calm as you tell the rules.

"The glass of water will touch only the paper. It won't rest on the rim of either of the other glasses. I won't move the other glasses. They will stay where they are. Even so, this piece of paper will hold the other glass up. The ends of the paper will touch the two glasses and there will not be any other supports."

Unless someone in the group is really very clever, no one will guess how you can do this. When you have built up the trick enough, it's time to take the spotlight and start your act.

Begin by folding the paper in an accordion fold along the long side. It looks ridged, instead of flat, like this:

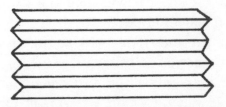

Now, rest the folded paper across the tops of the two glasses to make a bumpy "bridge." Very carefully, put the glass (with the water

in it) on the folded paper. Be sure it is correctly balanced; then let go. The paper will support it.

Practice this trick to be sure you're doing it correctly. It isn't a bad idea to use a plastic glass to hold the water for this balancing act.

Fork It Over

Cut a circle about three inches in diameter out of a piece of cardboard. Don't worry if it isn't a perfect circle.

Poke a hole in the middle of the circle and push a wooden pencil about halfway through. Don't worry if the hole isn't exactly at the midpoint of the circle.

Now, pretend you're trying to balance the pencil and cardboard circle on the end of your finger. When it keeps falling off, try the side of your finger. Naturally, the pencil won't balance.

Move the cardboard closer to the pencil's point. Try again. It still won't balance.

Insist you can make it balance. Offer to let others try. They will fail.

Now is the time to show your brilliant skill.

"I'll just add weight. Heavier things are easier to balance," you say.

Poke one tine of a dinner fork through the cardboard near one edge. Careful! First, you don't want to rip the cardboard. Second, you don't want to cut your finger!

Turn the contraption sideways, with the fork hanging from the lower edge of the circle. You are now ready for a surprising balancing act.

Rest the pointed end of the pencil flat along the tip of your finger. Slide the pencil

forward or backward until you can feel it is balanced. Let go and the whole thing will seem to hang in space.

You can change the way this device balances by slipping the cardboard nearer or farther from the pencil's point.

If you want to improve this trick, experiment with larger or smaller cardboard circles and longer or shorter pencils.

The Pickup Stunt

For this trick you need a Ping-Pong ball and a glass. The glass must bulge in the middle (see the sketch on page 71) or at the bottom. Place the ball under the glass on top of a table. Then stand back to admire your work, setting the stage for the stunt.

"Can you lift that ball off the table without touching *anything* besides the

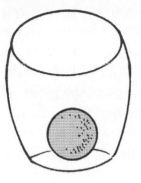

glass?" you ask. Go on to set a few rules. "But you can't slide the glass off the table so the ball falls to the floor. You must lift the ball, not drop it."

Like many good tricks, at first glance this one seems impossible, too. (Actually, it continues to look impossible at second or even third glance!)

Someone may try to lift the ball using static electricity from a comb, but this probably won't work. The ball is too heavy for that.

When showdown time arrives and your reputation is on the line, get a firm hold on the glass. Begin to move it in quick circles on the table. This will cause the ball to begin to circle the rim of the glass. Move the glass faster and the ball will pick up speed, too.

As the ball speeds up, it will start to climb the side of the glass. Since the glass bulges out wider in the middle than at the opening, the ball will begin to spin around the bulge.

(By the way, don't even bother trying this trick with a glass which does not bulge in the middle or at the bottom. It won't work.)

By now you will find you can move the glass back and forth in rapid little shakes of your hand and the ball will spin inside the bulge.

Gently lift the glass while you keep shaking it. The spinning ball comes off the table with the glass. You can continue shaking the glass and the ball will continue spinning until your hand gets tired.

A marble will also work in this trick. So will any small rubber, plastic or wooden ball. Just be sure to practice this trick in private until you know exactly how to get the ball spinning fast enough to lift it from the table.

When you complete this "impossible" trick, don't be overly modest. Take a few bows when your show is over.

Coin Push

If you don't mind getting downright sneaky, this quick trick is sure to catch someone. Like so many good con games, this one depends upon the use of words. People hearing your dare think one thing, while you have something else in mind.

You need an object, such as a large-size coin or a spoon, plus a ring. Hold up the ring and then place it next to the coin or spoon.

Say: "I can push that coin through this ring" or "I am sure I can push the spoon through the ring."

Let your victim examine both objects. Obviously, you have lost what little mind you once had, your shill will be thinking.

"I can do it," you insist.

When your friend insists you can't, it is time to get the show on the road.

Hold the ring in one hand next to the coin or spoon you are going to push. Stick one of the fingers of your other hand through the ring. Give the coin or spoon a push. That's all.

You may wish to add, "I just pushed the coin through the ring," but you probably won't have to explain yourself. The look on your victim's face usually lets you know you have scored again.

Showmanship—Plus Balance

Many tricks take a little showmanship to make them successful. In this one, most of the showmanship comes at the end of the performance. Not only does this trick *sound* impossible, it *looks* impossible when you've done it!

You need two dinner forks, an empty drinking glass, and a quarter. Oh, yes, don't forget the steady hands! You can use a cup or a mug, if you want, instead of a glass.

Begin by balancing the coin on the edge of the cup or glass—just to attract the attention of the onlookers. Then hold up the two forks, study the coin and glass, and begin your trickery with a talk:

"Someone told me it is possible to balance these two forks on that coin."

"Big deal," someone will probably reply.

"Yes, but I am supposed to do it so that

only the coin touches the glass. The two forks may touch each other and they must touch the coin. But only the coin is allowed to touch the rim of the glass."

"That isn't so hard," your victim may reply.

"But only the edge of the coin is allowed to touch the rim of the glass. And the forks may not touch that edge of the coin."

At this point, you have your victims hooked. It is time to allow them to try this impossible balancing act.

After everyone else gives up, show your stuff. Slip the coin between the first and second tines of the two forks. This leaves the handles of the forks pointing away from each other.

Here comes the tricky part—both for your audience and for you! Rest the edge of the coin on the rim of the glass so that the forks do not touch the glass. Carefully move the handles of the forks back and forth until the entire thing balances on the rim of the glass. The coin will stick out from the glass and the forks will appear to hang out in space. As you work to achieve a balance, you'll feel the proper place to hold the forks. This feeling will be in your fingers when you

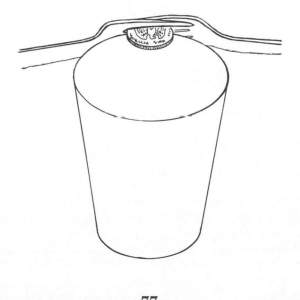

realize you no longer have to support the coin and forks.

Practice this trick before you show it. It takes steady hands and a little work, but it's worth it. Even when people see this balancing act, it's hard for them to believe their eyes.

PUZZLING NUMBERS, SNEAKY SHAPES

The Three-Penny Fooler

Hand your victim three pennies and say, "These are special pennies. They can communicate with my mind."

(Should anyone be rude enough to remark that your mind is only worth three cents, just ignore it. Remember, they laughed at Columbus.)

Then you give a very important command.

"Without letting me see, put some pennies in your right hand and the rest in your left."

When this is done, continue giving directions. "Mentally multiply the number of pennies in your right hand by three."

Pause while he or she multiplies. Then go on, "Now multiply the number of pennies in your left hand by four."

"Add the two products together and tell me the total," you say next.

When you hear the sum of the two numbers, you can tell at once which hand is holding the *odd number* of pennies. Tell your victim.

Here's how the trick works.

```
    L              R
    2              1
  x 4            x 3
  ___            ___
    8              3


        8
      + 3
      ____
      11 (odd)
```

Assume the right hand holds one penny: $3 \times 1 = 3$. Two pennies hidden in the left hand get multiplied by four; the product is eight. Add the sums: $8 + 3 = 11$.

Eleven is an *odd* number. Therefore, the right hand holds the odd number of pennies.

To make this trick seem even trickier than it is, change the multipliers the next time you give directions. Have your opponents multiply the number of pennies in their right hand by five. Then ask them to multiply the pennies in the left hand by two.

```
        L                       R
        2                       1
      x 2                     x 5
      ───                     ───
        4                       5

              4
            + 5
            ───
            9 (odd)
```

```
        L                    R
        0                    3
      x 0                  x 7
        0                   21
                0
             + 21
             21 (odd)
```

The thing to remember is always to use an *odd* number to multiply the pennies in the *right* hand. Use an *even* multiplier for the *left* hand.

If the final answer is odd, you'll know that the right hand holds an odd number of coins. If the final answer is even, the odd number of coins will be in the left hand.

Try this trick with five or seven or nine pennies instead of three. Just make sure your victim always has an *odd* number of coins. And always multiply the right hand by an odd number and the left by any even number.

What if your victim decides to put all the coins in one hand? No need to worry. Just make sure you always say, "Put *some* pennies in your right hand." Even if the left hand is empty the trick works. Suppose the three pennies in the right hand are multiplied by seven, and the empty left hand is multiplied by four: 3 x 7 = 21; 0 x 4 = 0. The sum of 21 + 0 equals an odd number. So you know the odd number of pennies must be in the right hand.

For Squares Only

Puzzles are fun, especially puzzles with a trick to them. The trick to solving this puzzle is for you to visualize squares differently—to think of squares in a manner other than a box.

Tell your victim: "I can make three squares exactly the same size using only eight lines. Four of these lines are exactly two inches long. The other four lines are exactly one inch long."

Just to be helpful, on a piece of paper, you can draw the lines you'll be using.

This puzzle doesn't seem difficult until people actually try to do it. It's hard for most people to change their ideas of a square!

When the time comes to prove that you're still the trickiest character around, draw the three squares resting on an angle, like these three diamond shapes, at the top of page 85.

Half and Half

The only trick to this little brainteaser is getting over the fact that it sounds impossible.

Tell your victim this story. (Make it longer and better, if you wish.)

"A grandmother saved her change to share with her three grandchildren. One day when all three of them visited her, she had collected some quarters to give them.

"Since she liked Janice best of all, she gave her half of all the quarters, plus half a quarter.

"She didn't like Howard quite as much, so she gave him half the quarters she had left, plus half a quarter.

"Finally she got to Tommy, who had broken her favorite vase during his last visit. Since she was still upset about his carelessness, she gave the unlucky boy half the quarters she had left, plus half a quarter.

"The grandmother didn't damage any of the coins, but she did give away all the quarters she had saved. How many quarters did she begin with? How many quarters did each grandchild receive?"

If your friends solve this one for you be sure to tell them how intelligent they are. (After all, no trick works *every* time, does it?)

If your friends give up, it's time for you to introduce some more tricky arithmetic.

The grandmother had seven quarters. Janice got half of seven plus a half. Half of seven is three and one-half; plus a half, it equals four. So Janice picked up four quarters as her share of the loot.

Howard received half of the three remaining quarters, plus a half. Half of three is one and one-half; plus a half, it makes two. This left the grandmother with only one quarter.

Poor Tommy was certainly sorry he broke his grandmother's favorite vase. He got half of that last quarter plus half a quarter, which left him with one quarter.

But when you think about it, one quarter is better than none.

Missing Money

Before presenting this listening problem to your friends it will be fun for you to read it through and try to solve it on your own. Then memorize it so you can boggle your friends.

Three friends decided to try out the new

All-You-Can-Eat Restaurant that just opened. They ate a fantastic meal—much more than they should have eaten.

"That will be $10 each," the cashier told them when they finally finished eating.

Each one of the three friends paid with a $10 bill.

It was only after they had left the restaurant that the cashier realized she had overcharged them. She remembered that the restaurant had a special price that night: $25 for three guests.

"Quick," she exclaimed, handing the waiter five $1 bills. "Run after those three people and give them their refund."

The waiter ran out of the restaurant and saw the three friends getting into their car. He waved to attract their attention. By the time he reached the car, the waiter knew he had a problem: There was no easy way to divide $5 evenly among three people!

"Wait," he said, panting. "The cashier overcharged you." He handed each of them a dollar bill. He kept the remaining $2 for himself.

"Thank you," one of the diners said to the waiter. To her friends she said, "This is great. It only cost us $9 each for that wonderful meal."

The three friends drove away thinking the meal cost them only $27 instead of $30.

The waiter was pleased because he had $2 in his pocket and a guilty conscience.

But wait! The three people paid $30 to begin with. With their refund, they really paid $27. The waiter has $2. Since 27 + 2 = 29, what happened to the missing dollar?

Nearly every time you tell this tricky story, you will fool most (if not all) of your listeners.

The trick lies in the way you figure things at the end. To have it make sense and to find the missing dollar, look at it this way:

Don't start by adding the waiter's $2 to the $27 the diners *thought* they paid. The waiter had tricked them by keeping some money, so they only should have paid $25. Remember? The cashier has $25. So you should begin by adding the waiter's $2 and the diners' $3 to the cashier's amount: 25 + 2 + 3 = 30.

Hurrah! The lost dollar has been found!

Moon Base

The nation's first base on the moon was being built at last. The first moon base consisted of six buildings. You can see the base layout on page 91.

The engineers have to connect the Heating to the Command Post, the Spaceship Hangar, and to the Living Quarters. Then the Power

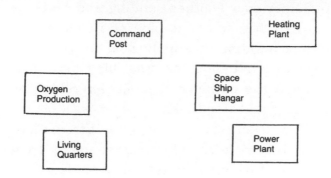

Plant must also be connected to the Command Post, the Spaceship Hangar, and the Living Quarters. Finally, Oxygen Production must also be connected to the Command Post, the Spaceship Hangar, and the Living Quarters.

At once, the engineers ran into problems. Their connecting pipes and lines may run in any direction and may be as long as needed. However, no pipe or line may cross any other pipe or line. No pipe or line may cross itself. Finally, no pipe or line may run through, under, or over another building and continue on. In other words, a pipe or line must go into a building to supply heat or power or oxygen. That pipe or line may not pass *through* the building. It must *connect to* the building and stop there.

Since there are to be only three pipes from the Heating Plant, three more from Oxygen Production, and three lines from the Power Plant, it looks like an easy job. It isn't. After weeks and months of trying, the engineers say the task is impossible. And they are correct! There is no way to set up the moon base under the conditions given.

You don't believe it is impossible? No one does. The task looks too simple to be impossible. Try it. Then try it again. Try it as many times as you wish. You will never be able to connect the final pipe or line. After you've found that it really is not possible, then spring this one on others.

Lucky Number Seven

"Seven is my lucky number," you may tell someone. "In fact, every time I do a math problem, the answer comes up seven."

Before anyone has a chance to prove this is not so, begin this number trick.

"Choose a number," you tell your victim. "Any number. Just don't tell me what it is."

When this is done, you say, "Add nine to the number you just chose."

"Now multiply that total by two," you continue, when the addition is completed.

"Subtract four from the number you got when you multiplied," you say for the next step.

"Divide that answer by two," you suggest next.

The trick is nearly finished now. For the last step you direct, "Subtract the number you started with."

Watch as the truth dawns on your victim. "See?" you will probably say. "What did I tell you? The answer is seven, isn't it?"

Let's practice this trick, just to make sure it works. Begin with number 20.

$$
\begin{array}{r}
20 \\
+\ 9 \\
\hline
29
\end{array}
\text{ x 2 = 58}
$$

$$
\begin{array}{r}
58 \\
-\ 4 \\
\hline
54
\end{array}
\text{ / 2 = 27}
$$

$$
\begin{array}{r}
27 \\
-\ 20 \\
\hline
7
\end{array}
$$

How about that?

Five Is a Tricky Number

This quick mental math trick works every time.

Have your victim write a number on a piece of paper, keeping it out of your sight.

"Now add seven to that number," you say.

"Take the total you just got and multiply that by two," you command for the next step.

"Now subtract four from the product when you multiplied."

When this is done, you tell your victim, "Divide the subtraction answer by two."

"Subtract the number you started with," you continue.

When the math work is all finished, pretend to think for a few seconds. Then grin and announce, "Your final answer is five."

This is always true with this tricky number problem when the math is done exactly this way. Let's zip through it just to see that it works.

Starting with:

$$
\begin{array}{r}
12 \\
+\ 7 \\
\hline
19
\end{array}
\ \text{x}\ 2 = 38
$$

$$
\begin{array}{r}
38 \\
-\ 4 \\
\hline
34
\end{array}
\ /\ 2 = 17
$$

$$
\begin{array}{r}
17 \\
-\ 12 \\
\hline
5
\end{array}
$$

Memorize the commands. Then try this one on your math teacher!

Four from Four Leaves Eight

Hand a square or rectangular sheet of paper to a friend. Pass along a pencil as well.

"I bet I can take four from four and leave eight," you tell your friend. "See whether or not you can. If you can't, then I'll show you how it's done."

Of course, your friend will try all sorts of solutions. Roman numerals. Fractions. Unless your friend comes up with some fancy math as yet unknown, though, there isn't a chance in the world you'll meet up with an answer to this stumper.

When your friend finally gives up, it is time for you to shine. Take back the paper and point out that it has four corners. Next, tear off each corner, as shown on page 98.

While your friend is still sputtering, say, "There were four corners. I took those four corners away. Now there are eight corners left on the paper."

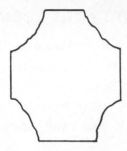

It is probably best that you not say anything more at this time. Chances are you've said enough.

Last One Loses

This game has been played for years and years. It looks simple but makes a great trick once you know its secret. Begin by making sixteen marks on a piece of paper or a blackboard so they look like rows of capital I's, as shown on page 99.

The object of the game is to cross off

marks, either one, two, or three marks at a time. Players take turns and the player who crosses off the last mark loses.

Naturally, there is a way to change this from a game of sheer luck into a contest of skill. All it takes is a little quick counting. Make sure you always leave your opponent with thirteen, nine, and five marks to remove—and finally just one. It is that simple: Just remember the numerals 13, 9, 5, and 1.

If you go first, you can always win. Just

take away three marks and then, no matter what your opponent marks off, cross out enough to leave exactly nine marks. Next turn, leave your victim with five and no matter what your opponent's next move is, you can arrange things so your rival must cross off the last mark.

When your opponent begins play, keep the numerals 13, 9, 5, and 1. Do your best to leave the other player facing these numbers. Once you can do this...it's as easy as 1-2-3!

Not Just for Squares

Everybody is always looking for a trick that can be done easily. This one should fill the bill.

Draw a square. The trick is to divide the square into as many pieces as possible by drawing just four straight lines. Each line must extend from one side of the square to

any other side. Don't sneak a peek at the answer on page 102 and you can try this trick on yourself first.

Here's a hint to get you started: You can make *more* than eight pieces inside, using just four lines. So keep trying until you are sure you've done it. Then, and only then, should you check the answer to see how well you have really done.

When you make this dare to others, you are usually on pretty safe ground. Not many people see the right answer without giving the square quite a bit of study.

Turn the page upside down for the answer.

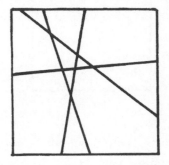

Eleven pieces is the best possible effort. Do it like this.

Drive Them Dotty

Draw the group of spots shown on page 103, on a piece of paper. Dare a friend to connect all nine by drawing five straight lines—never lifting the pencil from the paper once the drawing begins. Drawing can begin at any point but ends after only five straight lines.

Of course your friend can do this in an instant. It is almost too easy to be worth doing.

While your friend is still basking in the warm glow of success, make your bet.

Tell your successful friend, "I'll bet you can't connect the same set of dots without raising your pencil from the paper and by drawing only *four* straight lines this time. What's more, I bet I can."

Who can turn down an easy dare like that? Especially after just having met your first dare, it is all but impossible to resist. You know the secret—four moves is many times harder than five.

Try doing this in four moves before looking for victims.

Turn the page upside down for the answer.

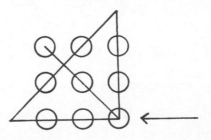

I Win—You Lose

Everyone likes to be a winner. With this little arithmetic game, chances are good you'll be one.

The object of the game is for each player to write or say a number from one to six, which is then added to a growing list. First one says or writes a number, then the other player. Each new number suggested is added to the previous number. The player who adds the number that brings the total to 30 is the winner.

Here's one way the game could go:

Opponent writes the numeral 5.

You write 4, which brings the total to 9.

Opponent writes 3, for a total of 12.

You write 4, bringing the total to 16.

Opponent writes 1, for a total of 17.

You write 6, making a total of 23.

At this point your opponent looks sick. If he adds one you will choose six. Should he select two, you will choose five. If he goes for three, you'll choose four and so on. The game is yours.

Let's run through another game, just to be sure you have it well in mind.

You begin by writing the numeral 2.

Your opponent writes 3, for a total of 5.

You write 4 to bring the total to 9.

Opponent writes 3, for a 12 total.

You add 4 to make the total 16.

Opponent writes 5, which brings the total to 21.

You write 2, for a total of 23.

Again, your opponent is beaten. No matter what number your opponent adds, from one to six, you will be able to bring the total to 30 with your next number. You win again. Lucky you!

Well, not lucky exactly. Look back over the two games illustrated. Figure out the secret of play. Then check your idea with the solution on this page.

Once you're sure of yourself, go in search of opponents. So long as you play with care you will win far more often than you'll lose.

Unbeatable totals are ones with the numerals 9, 16, 23, and 30—but the key is being the one to write 9. Then the rest fall into place.

That's simple if you start. Write the numeral 2 or higher and you can easily finagle the next few moves. But if your opponent begins, it's trickier. If your opponent writes a numeral 3 or higher, add 6 to go to 9 at once. If your opponent writes a 1 or 2 to start, just add a 1. Then keep an eye out for trouble. If your opponent adds 6, write 1 to being the total to 10. Then, if your opponent chooses anything besides 6, you will still be able to be the one to reach the next critical numeral: 16.

If you start, begin with the numeral 2. Your opponent's number can't bring the written total to 9 but whatever you add next can do it.

The only time you are in danger of losing is when your opponent begins by writing 1 or 2. Even then, you'll only lose if your opponent knows the secret—or has a lot of luck!

Count Down

All our lives we put things in their proper order. By now, you should be an expert at putting numbers in order. Study the column of numbers below. Believe it or not, the numbers in the column are arranged in their proper order, though it may not be an order familiar to you at first. As you can see, most of the numbers between one and fifteen are here. Only the numerals 4 and 9 are not in the column.

After you have decided why the numbers are arranged as they are, put 4 and 9 in their correct places.

After you have decided where to place the numerals 4 and 9, check the solution just to

8
11
15
5
14
1
7
6
10
13
3
12
2

make certain you figured out the pattern. Then try this one on your friends. For such a plain little puzzle it fools almost everyone who tries it.

Turn the page upside down for the answer.

The numbers are in alphabetical order. Four should follow five and nine comes after fourteen.

What a Shot!

The archery target shown on this page isn't the everyday target used in archery class. But it is a target that should help you win a bet or two.

Here's your dare. You are willing to bet that an archer can shoot six arrows into the target and get a score of exactly one hundred. None of the six arrows will miss the target. All will hit a scoring ring. And the score will be exactly 100.

Can you win your own bet now? Don't be too quick to check the upside-down answer. This one is a bit hard to imagine, but it is possible.

Turn the page upside down for the answer.

Try placing two arrows in the 16 ring and four in the 17 ring.

What's Next?

All your friends *think* they know how to count. Here is a listening stunt that puts a person's counting skill to the test.

Challenge someone to tell you what number comes next or follows each number you say. Be sure to tell the person to answer quickly. This, of course, keeps them from having enough time to stop and think.

Begin by saying, "19."

Naturally, your opponent will answer, "20."

Then you say, "186."

Next say, "294."

Then say, "567."

Go on to say, "1026."

Say next, "2169."

Then say, "4099."

Here is where you win or lose. If you've been saying numbers rapidly, the chances are good that the person you are playing against will say "5000" when you say "4099," instead of 4100. Try this with a few people and see if this isn't the case.

You don't need to memorize the numbers given above. Just start with small numbers and work up to larger ones. Be sure that the final number you use is 4099, or 5099, or 6099 and so forth.

Put on Your Thinking Cap

You don't have to be a great mathematician in order to come up with the answer to this poser. In spite of this, lots and lots of people don't see how to arrive at the proper answer.

The average human head contains around 125,000 hairs. Absolutely no human head contains as many as 499,999 hairs.

A huge open-air concert was held. Exactly 500,000 people attended. No one who came to the concert was totally bald. Is it possible that no two people attending the concert had exactly the same number of hairs on their heads?

See if your answer matches this one before giving this little problem to others:

It is not possible that no two people had the same numbers of hairs on their heads. If no head ever has as many as 499,999 hairs and 500,000 people were present, one (and very likely many) pair of people had to have the same number of hairs, since every possible number of hairs from 1 to 499,999 is covered.

Checkerboard Squares

Who hasn't played checkers or at least looked at a checkerboard? But how many people have ever tried to count all the squares on a checkerboard? Few have. Fewer still have counted correctly.

A checkerboard has eight squares on a side. Since eight times eight equals sixty-four, then there must be 64 squares on a checkerboard, right? Wrong.

The entire board is a square, so that adds at least one more. And what about all the squares within the board which are formed when you consider two-by-two squares to make a larger square? And how about the three-by-three squares or those four-by-four, and so on? Don't forget that the larger squares may overlap one another.

Begin by counting the number of squares for yourself. Work it out by yourself and then rework it just to be on the safe side. Be sure you count just squares, not rectangles that aren't squares. Are you ready to check your answer with the one given below?

Once you're positive you've located all those elusive squares, it is time to dare some unsuspecting friend to count them. Very few people arrive at the right number on the first try.

Turn the page upside down for the answer.

There are 204 squares on the checkerboard:

1 by 1 = 64	*2 by 2 = 49*	*3 by 3 = 36*
4 by 4 = 25	*5 by 5 = 16*	*6 by 6 = 9*
7 by 7 = 4	*8 by 8 = 1*	

Note that all the totals (64, 49, 36, etc.) are square numbers

Count the Rectangles

When you bet someone they can't correctly count the number of rectangles in the figure below they are likely to accept your bet. Why don't you try the dare first?

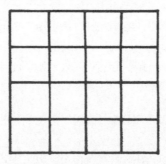

Remind your victim that all squares are rectangles and that rectangles come in a variety of sizes. So, two squares next to each other form a third rectangle together in this figure. Do three squares in a line. For that matter, a rectangle that is two squares by three squares can be found in several locations in the figure. And don't forget overlapping rectangles.

There's no sneaky trick to it, but try this one first before daring others to count the rectangles.

Here's a hint. Set up a list of all the possible rectangles in the figure, under groupings like "2 by 2" or "3 by 2." Count all the rectangles of each size and record that number. Do one size at a time. Don't be too quick to think you've counted all the rectangles.

The upside-down answer indicates there are quite a few hidden in the figure-maybe more than you guessed!

Answer on next page.

There are 100 rectangles in the figure.

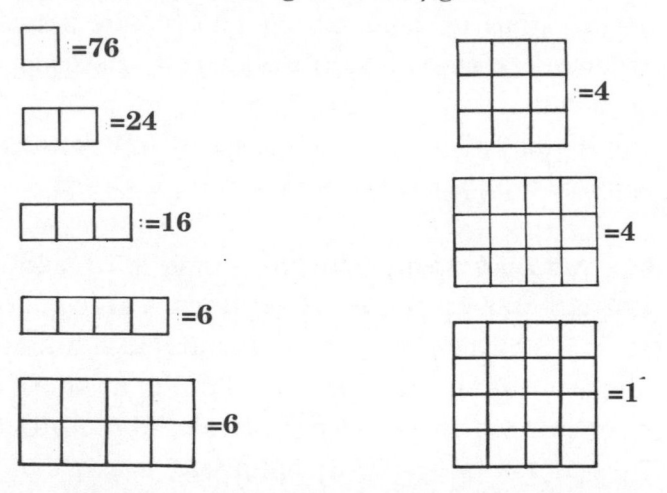

☐ =76

☐☐ =24

☐☐☐ :=16

☐☐☐☐ =6

☐☐☐☐ (2×4) =6

(3×3) =4

(3×4) =4

(4×4) =1

STUNT PERSON

Hands Off

Here's one that is *sooooo* easy it seems it must be hard. Try challenging yourself first. Begin by placing any item in your right hand.

A coin, a toy, a book—anything is just fine. Stand with your arms stretched straight out to the sides.

With both arms still outstretched, move the object from your right hand to your left. Do it without bending your elbows. Don't bring your arms together. Don't bend your wrists.

Above all, don't give up too quickly.

It is really quite easy once you figure it out. Simply tilt your body over *sideways* to place the object on the table using one outstretched arm. Then, with your arms still unbending, turn around and tilt over the other way to pick up the object with your other hand. Hands down, this is the easiest trick to pull on a friend.

A Difficult Burden

You can play this as a quick bet or spend a lot of time giving it a big, fancy buildup. Either way you'll have a winning stunt.

It goes like this: "I bet I can find something for you to hold in your right hand that you can't hold in your left no matter how strong you are."

You can draw things out by talking about a newspaper article you just read that explains how people can hold much more weight in one hand than in another. You may even invent a long story about possible reasons why people can hold more weight in their right hands than in their left. That's up to you.

At any rate, once your dare has been accepted, take the person's right hand in yours and move it so it is holding the opposite elbow.

You can then say, "You are now holding

your left elbow in your right hand. Can you hold your left elbow in your left hand?"

It's impossible, of course, and you've won.

More Difficult than It Looks

Choose your opponent carefully for this trick. It is a good one, because it's more difficult than it seems to be at first. Only a few people may be strong enough to defeat you.

When an opponent does get the better of you, always remember to be gracious and congratulate that individual. After all, it pays to be polite to people who are stronger than you.

To set this trick up, stand straight. Put the palm of your hand on the top of your head. You may even pretend your hand is stuck there, if you want to.

"Can you help me lift my hand off my

head?" you ask. "Just push up on my forearm, please."

Naturally, you will push down as hard as you can. The trick comes when someone tries to lift up on your forearm to remove your hand.

It is much harder than you'd expect it to be.

To increase your odds, stand so that your opponent is lifting with an outstretched arm. Don't let anyone get under your arm and push straight up.

Ready, Set, Jump

Some tricks work best on people who think they are wonderful math students. Others are designed to lure great athletes. This one is for the athletes.

To set up the trick, stand in the middle of

a room and pretend to practice jumping backward. Don't do it very well. It won't take long for your victim to start feeling superior and begin showing you how it should be done. Or your victim may just make fun of your attempts. Either way you have hooked a stooge. That's what counts.

Ask your victim to show you how to jump backward. Or you might want to pretend you resent being kidded about your lack of ability. Take the approach that suits you best.

Whichever you choose, say, "Sure. You can jump backward when there's nothing to jump over. I'll bet if I put this book on the floor you can't jump over it backward." Hold up a small book.

What athlete can turn down a challenge like that?

"Look," you may go on, "I don't want to make you look bad. But I know if I put this book down you can't jump over it backward."

By now your victim is ready to jump the moon if only given the chance.

"Let's get this straight. I say I can put the book down on the floor and you can't jump over it backward. Just one thing. After I put it on the floor, you can't move it. Not even an inch. Is it a deal?"

Of course it's a deal.

Walk to the nearest corner in the room and put the book in that corner. Make certain it touches both walls. Then step back and point to the book.

You may even wish to say something pleasant such as, "we are waiting" or "happy landing."

Jump Across the Room

Before everyone has recovered from your last trick, pull this one. Everyone will know this is another trick. Unless someone is pretty sharp, though, you'll be able to pull this one off just as easily as the others.

"I can jump across the room faster than you," you'll say, pointing to a distant corner. This is sure to grab attention. Make sure it is a fairly big room you are in.

You are sure to be asked to make your move by at least one person.

Tell your opponent to go first. Make a big deal about timing the challenger's attempt. When it's your turn to jump across the room, just run from one side of it to the other. Once there, jump up and down a few times on the far side. You have jumped across the room just as you said you would.

You may want to say something such as,

"See, it isn't all that hard. *You* can probably do it with a little practice."

Lead Foot

It can be upsetting from time to time to find out that you cannot do the simplest of things. For victims of this trick, it's another of those times.

Tell an audience of friends that you can make it impossible for someone to jump even a few inches off the floor. Promise you won't touch the person, who will be allowed to stand apart. There won't be anything heavy to hold, either.

Of course, there is one little catch. The person trying to jump must stand with his or her back to a wall. Heels, hips, and shoulders must touch the wall. Then, without bending or leaning forward, the victim must try to jump.

It just isn't possible, not in the position just described. You'll have tried it yourself, of course, so you'll know that's certain. See just how many people will jump at the chance to try it themselves.

Sit This One Out

You don't have to rehearse this stunt to get it right the first time. Just tell someone, "I bet I can find a place in this room where I can sit, but you can't."

Who can turn down a dare like that?

First, sit in a chair.

Naturally, after you get up, your victim will sit in the same chair. Scratch your head and mutter that you'll have to keep looking.

Next, you might sit on the floor. Your victim will sit on the floor exactly where you did.

This can go on for as long as you wish to stretch out the stunt; have your victim sit in a chair, on a sofa, or wherever you wish. Finally, make your move before your victim gets up from one of the places.

Sit in the person's lap.

There shouldn't be a bit of doubt; you have won your bet. If there is any question, dare the victim to sit in his or her own lap. You know it can't be done.

Brute Force

When you tell people that you'll be able to push their hands apart—no matter how hard they try to hold them together—you'll find many who will take your dare. One is all you'll need for this trick.

Have your opponent make two fists then set one fist on top of the other and hold them firmly together. Tell the person to press those fists together tightly.

Flex a few muscles then brag, "I bet I can push your hands apart using only one finger from each hand." Then do so.

Simply put the index finger (the pointer finger) of each hand on the back of both fists of your opponent and push sharply sideways. The two fists will separate. Try it out first on a good friend and see that it's true.

Here's a little trick you may want to work into your act. You may want to bet that your opponent can't push your fists apart. If you decide to go this route, here's what you have to do. Direct attention away with loud talk or a gesture so no one sees your next move: As you place your two fists together, let the thumb on your bottom fist stick up. Wrap the fingers of your top fist around that thumb.

Now your two fists are locked firmly together.

If you run into someone whose fists you can't push apart, chances are excellent that you're pushing against a fist which contains the thumb of the other fist. Check to be sure you're not up against a rival trickster!

Hands Down

Here is just the thing for taking on tough guys who think they can do anything. Before showing this stunt to anyone else though, try it yourself.

Begin by placing your hand on a table so that the tips of all four fingers and your thumb can press down firmly. Bend the middle finger under so that the top joint rests firmly on the tabletop as well.

Keeping your fingers pressed down on the

table, lift your thumb an inch or so from the tabletop. Return it to its position pressing down. Lift the forefinger an inch and return it. Do the same with the little finger. Nothing to it, is there?

There is! With the thumb, fingertips, and the middle finger's knuckle still pushing down firmly on the table, try to lift your ring finger. It can't be done! So long as the joint of the middle finger, your thumb, and your other fingertips press down, you simply can't lift the tip of your ring finger from the top of the table.

Don't strain and struggle because you might make your hand sore if you try too hard for too long a time.

Once you have found how impossible this stunt is, you'll be raring to try it on your friends. Watch the surprised looks on their faces as people try to do what seems very easy but is anything but.

Act Like a Flamingo

Flamingos are those big, pink birds you see in zoos. One interesting thing about flamingos is that so many of them stand around on one leg. But even a flamingo couldn't do this trick.

Is there any place in the room you can't stand on one leg for even as little as five seconds? There is.

Stand with one side against the wall. Be sure your shoulder and the side of your foot touch the wall. Now lift the other foot from the floor and try to remain standing. Try is all you can do. You'll find you can't remain standing in this position no matter how hard you work at it.

After you're sure that this is impossible, it is time to go in search of victims. Issue your dare by saying, "I bet I can find a place in this room where you can't stand on one leg!"

When your dare is accepted, do your stuff. You've just made a sure bet.

Easy Money

Everyone likes a chance to earn some easy money. Here is a stunt that looks like a quick way to pick up a coin, but isn't. Try this yourself before daring others because you won't believe it's so tricky.

Have your victim stand with both heels against the wall. Place a coin on the floor about two feet in front of your friend's toes.

Tell your friend to pick up the coin without moving either heel away from the wall. Also, warn your friend not to lift either heel from the floor.

Keeping heels on the floor *and* against the

wall, none of your friends will be able to bend over or kneel down to pick up the coin.

Still don't believe it? As easy as this seems, it is impossible to do.

GRAB A GLASS

Huff and Puff

Lots of tricks use common items like drinking glasses and old soda bottles. For this trick just turn an empty soda bottle on its side. Crush a small piece of paper into a tight wad. You're ready.

Choose a victim who is a real braggart and deserves to be squelched.

"Look closely," you say, as you begin. "I am putting this wad of paper right here in the open end of the bottle."

You continue, "What I want you to do is to blow the paper into the bottle with only one

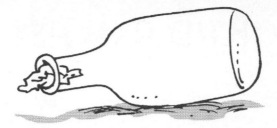

breath of air. Now, just to be fair, I need to warn you of something. This is very difficult. Most people just can't blow hard enough to do it.

"Get a deep breath. Then *blow really hard*. Just remember you only get one try, so make that first blast of air do the trick."

By now, you have your victim convinced it is necessary to blow for all he or she is worth. What happens when the victim blows hard is a real surprise.

The paper wad does not go into the bottle. It does just the opposite. It flies out into the face of the huffer and puffer. The harder he or she blows, the faster the paper wad shoots out of the bottle.

This trick depends upon a hard blast of air. That is why you need to stress how hard the victim must blow. A tiny little dribble of air may allow the paper wad to slip into the bottle.

This trick really takes the wind out of a person's sails.

Pretty Sneaky

The first part of this trick is just a good test of logic and planning. The second part is downright sneaky. That's what makes it such a great trick.

Arrange five empty glasses as shown at the top of the next page, alternating up, down, up, down, up. (The numbers are there just to help explain how to do the steps.)

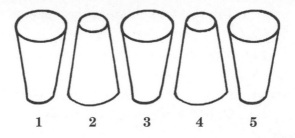

1   2   3   4   5

"Here's the trick," you tell your audience. "I am going to turn over two glasses at a time. I will do this three times. At the end of three turns, all five glasses will be right side up."

This doesn't sound all that difficult, so no one will act wildly impressed. Don't let this bother you. Just show everyone that you can do what you said you'd do.

Turn over glasses 1 and 4.

Turn over glasses 2 and 5.

Turn over glasses 1 and 5.

That's all there is to it. All five glasses are now sitting with their tops up.

You may want to say something like, "I told you I could do it." While you're talking, begin rearranging the glasses as casually as possible.

If anyone says something about how easy the trick was, you have a new pigeon. Otherwise, when the glasses are set up again, dare someone to do what you just did in three moves.

Strangely enough, *it is impossible for another person to repeat what they just saw you do*. No matter how many times people try, the trick won't work.

When you are asked for a repeat performance, you have to decide whether to risk

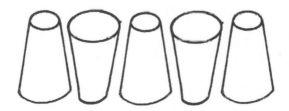

giving away the trick or not. If you set up the glasses *after* someone has failed and the glasses are rearranged, the chances are good you won't get caught.

Here is the sneaky part of this trick. When you position the glasses for someone else, always arrange them like this: glass down, up, down, up, down.

To most people, this arrangement looks exactly like the one you began with. Of course, it isn't, which is what makes the trick work.

If you decide to risk showing the solution again, keep up a steady stream of talk while you set up the glasses properly. Your talk may help to distract your audience from noticing how the glasses are arranged.

A Person Could Die of Thirst

Here's a good one to tone down hotshots who act as if they know more than anyone else.

Fill a plastic glass partly full of water, a soft drink, or whatever. Place an unbreakable saucer or salad plate on top of it. Then stand a second glass (an empty one) on the saucer. Hand this stack to your victim, making sure it's always held by the bottom glass.

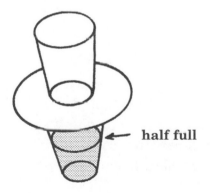

← half full

You say: "Don't touch either the top glass or the saucer with your hands, lips, teeth, or any other part of your body. You may touch anything else in the room but not those two items. Don't ask anyone else to touch the top glass or saucer until you're willing to admit you can't do this trick."

Present the challenge: "What you have to do is take a drink out of the bottom glass. But you must not let go of that bottom glass until you figure out how to take a drink from it."

Now you can give your victim a sly smile and boast, "Of course, if you can't figure out how to do it, I'll be happy to show you."

As is the case with most tricks, the solution is so easy and so obvious everyone wonders why they didn't see it first.

Position two boxes or two stacks of books side by side. Leave just enough room between them so you can lower the bottom glass in the space. Make certain the edges of the saucer or salad plate touch each stack firmly. Also, be sure the boxes or books are the same height.

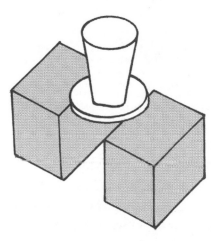

Once you have the saucer firmly settled on top of the boxes, remove the bottom glass and take a drink.

When someone says, "That's simple" or "That's easy," just smile. After all, if the answer was so simple, why didn't they think of it?

It's All in the Wrist

Set a soda bottle on a table. Actually, any bottle will work that has a narrow top about the size of a soda bottle.

Tear a strip about an inch wide from the long end of a sheet of notebook paper. Rest one end on top of the bottle.

Stack four coins on the strip of paper over the bottle. Make certain the larger coins are on the bottom if there is a difference in sizes. Three coins will work just as well as four.

Next, suggest that it is easy to pull the paper out from under the coins without spilling the coins.

Be sure to add, "Don't touch the coins or the bottle."

No matter how careful people are when they try this, the coins usually fall off the paper and bottle onto the table.

When everyone is pretty certain it can't be done it's your chance to come to the rescue.

Hold the loose end of the paper strip firmly in one hand. Bring the other hand down as fast as possible near the middle of the paper strip.

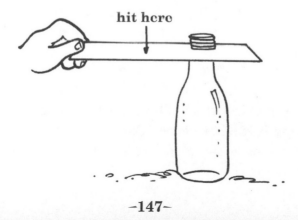

hit here

The sudden jerk will whip the paper out from under the coins. They will stay on top of the bottle. You will still be holding the paper strip by one end.

Sunken Treasure

If you have a steady hand and a bit of patience, this stunt should be right up your alley. Begin by filling a glass with water, right to the brim. Next, you need a handful of pennies. Dimes will do fine, but pennies are easier to get and you'll need lots of them.

The question is: How many pennies can you drop into the glass without having the water run over? Remember, the glass is already full of water. Can you drop in one coin before the glass runs over? How about two? Five? Ten?

Now test your guess; you're likely to be surprised. Drop the coins one at a time, waiting until each coin has settled to the bottom of the glass before dropping the next. Drop the coins as gently as possible. Let the surface of the water become calm before dropping the next one. Be careful not to touch the water with your fingers when releasing the coins.

As more and more coins plop into the glass full of water an interesting thing happens. The water will actually begin to rise above the edge of the glass. Eventually, you will be able to see the water bulging higher than the glass that is holding it. This has to do with something called the *surface tension* of the water, which holds it together even when it's stretched more than seems possible.

There is no exact number of coins you can drop into a full glass of water. It depends upon the size of the glass, among other things. Just don't be surprised if you run out of money before the water runs over!

When you have practiced a few times and know a safe number of coins for your glass, you're ready to go in search of a victim. Show that person the full glass of water and your handful of coins. Say something like, "I bet I can drop all these pennies into that glass of water without having the water run over."

When your victim says, "No way!" or something of the sort, you're ready to once again prove you can do what seems impossible.

If you really get into this stunt, you might want to try dropping straight pins into the water instead of coins. If you do, just be sure you have lots of time, plus lots and lots of pins... and patience.

By a Waterfall

Fill a glass full of water right up to the brim. Over the top of the glass, rest a small piece of thin cardboard. (A corner cut from a file folder is perfect.)

Now comes the dare. Suggest to a friend that you plan to turn the filled glass upside down while holding the cardboard in place. Add that you will then take your hand away from the cardboard. When you do this, tell your friend that you think the water will remain inside the upside-down glass.

Your victim may tell you that you'll be making a waterfall instead!

If you do the stunt carefully, you'll be a sure winner. But first, a warning: Practice this over the kitchen sink several times. Be sure the glass is completely full to the brim. Also be sure the cardboard is sealed tightly to the rim by the water when you turn the glass over. Finally, take your hand away from the cardboard slowly once you have the glass upside down.

What is called *atmospheric pressure* will hold the cardboard in place since the weight of the air pushing up is greater than the weight of the water pushing down. It's invisible, but air has a lot of power. This only works, however, so long as you don't let the cardboard pull away from the rim of the glass before you let go of the cardboard. If you're not careful, this dare can be a real workout.

Bottoms Up

This is a good one for a hot summer day but it gets them any time, every time.

Pick up a cup of water, iced tea, soda, or whatever you are drinking. (A can or bottle of soft drink works just as well.) Study the container of liquid in front of your selected stooges. Then finger the material of your shirt.

When you have everyone's attention, it's time to tell them, "I bet I can pour this drink down my neck without getting my shirt wet."

It will seem like a good idea to others even if the only gain is seeing you make a mess of yourself. But you'll know better.

When the dare has been agreed upon, all you have to do to win is drink whatever's in your cup. Then you've poured it down your neck, haven't you? And unless someone tries to douse you for setting them up, your shirt won't be even damp from your efforts.

An Impossible Test of Strength

At some time or another all of us have met people who seem just *too* perfect—or just think they are. This test of strength has been designed for the person with superhuman strength or the person who never seems to stop bragging about him- or herself.

Fill a glass nearly full of water. A plastic glass is safer to use than one made of breakable glass. Go up to your victim with the glass of water upright on the palm of your hand. Hold your arm straight out with the water glass balanced in your hand.

Tell Superkid, "I bet you can't hold this glass of water in the palm of your hand with your arm straight out from your shoulder just as mine is now. At least, you can't do it for more than just a few minutes."

Now who can turn down a challenge like that? Certainly not Superkid. Try to get your victim to set the amount of time he or she will hold the glass. The longer, the better. Five minutes is great. Seven or eight minutes are even better. Be sure the arm is extended straight out from the shoulder. Don't allow the victim to bend his or her elbow while holding the glass. After a couple of minutes you'll be able to see the strain. Most people give up long before five minutes pass. No one ever lasts as much as seven or eight minutes. (If you run into a victim who does survive that long, the chances are you've just run into the world's next champion...something!)

Even when not used as a putdown, this is a good stunt. It looks easy but quickly proves otherwise, though it won't seem so fast, to an unsuspecting pigeon struggling to hold up.

Don't Hang Up

For this puzzler you need a cup and a piece of string about four feet long. Don't use your family's best china for this stunt. A plastic, unbreakable cup is far better in case things go wrong.

Double the string so that it is now two feet long. Push the looped end of the string through the cup's handle. When the loop pops out the other side of the handle, poke the loose ends of the string through the loop. Tie the loose ends to a hook, a door-knob, a cupboard handle, or other secure object.

Now for the challenge. Can you remove the cup from the string without cutting the string, unfastening the string from where it's tied, or breaking the cup?

Try it. It is not at all hard.

When you bet people you can do this

stunt, don't let them handle the cup or the string. Let them look at it without trying it for themselves. Then show them you can win yet another bet: Just pull the center of the loop upward until you've made the loop bigger than the cup. Pass the cup through the enlarged loop and the cup is free. Don't drop it!

Be Quick About It

This stunt, which requires changing the order of things, is another that lots of people make much harder than it is.

Begin by setting up six glasses in a line. The first three glasses contain water. The next three are empty.

The trick is to move the six glasses around so that every other one is *full*. In other words, put the six glasses in a new order so that the first glass is full, the second is empty, the third is full, and so on.

There's a catch. Do this in the least possible number of moves, counting as a move each time you touch a glass or change its position. Take enough time to think this problem through before making your first move. You may want to try it a number of times just to be certain you are making the change in the least number of moves.

When you are sure you've done it, check the answer with this simple one: Pour the second glass into the fifth in one simple move.

See? Not so hard! And now you are ready to dare others to a contest. Explain the object of the puzzle and defy them to make the change in fewer moves than you. This is a contest you can't lose. A very, very few people may be able to make the change in the same number of moves as you do. No one will ever make it in *less*! That's a promise.

CONS WITH CARDS AND DICE

Pick a Card

You don't need to practice this card trick more than once or twice. It is easy to do, works every time, and fools most people time after time.

Hand your victim a deck of cards and say something like, "Pick a card, and don't let me see the card you pick. Just make sure you look at it long enough to remember which card it is. While you're looking at it, your brain waves will tell me which card it is."

This remark will probably invite some laughs and rude remarks, but don't pay any attention. Your time is coming.

"Now," you instruct your victim, "put the card you chose on top of the deck."

When this is done, you continue, "Now cut the deck."

This buries the chosen card somewhere in the middle of the deck.

After just one cut, pick up the deck of cards and begin taking the cards off and turning them over one at a time. When you reach the proper card you should hesitate, pretend to think, then say, "This is the card you chose."

Of course, you have picked the proper card and your victim wonders how. Offer to do it again. It works every time.

What makes this such a good trick is that it's so simple most people can't figure it out. They try to find a difficult answer instead of watching what you do.

What you must do at the start of the trick is see what card is on the very *bottom* of the deck. It is easy to do this when you first hand the deck to your victim.

When the victim chooses a card, that card goes on *top* of the deck. Then the deck is cut and the bottom stack of cards goes on top. This puts the bottom card right on top of the card your victim picked.

So when you start sorting through the deck, the bottom card—which you already recognize—will come right before the chosen card. It's as easy as that!

For variety, you may want to go past the correct card for a few cards and then return to it. In such a case, you might say, "Wait. Something is wrong here. Your brain waves are telling me I've gone too far." Then slowly go back through the cards and find the proper one.

Since you are the star of this act, it's up

to you how much of a show you want to put on. It is not magic but most people can't ever figure out how the trick works.

Dice-Reading Trick

Hand a friend four dice (they don't have to be the same size or color). Tell your friend to examine the dice carefully; then stack them, one die on top of the other. (One is a die; two or more are dice, by the way.)

You say: "I will turn my back while you stack the four dice. Then, when I turn around, I am going to look very closely at the one on top. I will not touch any of them.

"Using just the power of my mind I can see through the dice in the stack. This will allow me to tell you the total number of spots on all the hidden sides of the dice."

Even if you are using clear dice, this is

obviously impossible. There is no way you could see the spots on the seven hidden sides of all four dice.

Turn around and let your friend go to work. When it's time to do your mind reading you may want to make a production out of it. Peer closely. Look puzzled. Chant magic words. Do whatever makes the trick more dramatic. Then give the correct answer.

Here's how it works. Just subtract the number of spots on the top die from 28. The difference will be the total of the spots on the seven hidden sides (or faces) of the dice in the stack.

If the top has three spots, for example, seven hidden sides total 25. If a five is showing, the hidden sides total 23, and so on.

Why does that always work? Because the opposite sides of a die always add up to seven. Check one just to make sure. Six is always opposite one. Five is opposite two, and three and four are opposite each other.

Knowing this, you can see how this mind reading—or dice reading—trick works. The top and bottom face of each die must add up to seven. There are four dice: 4 x 7 = 28. Subtract the value of the top face from 28 and you have the total for the seven hidden faces.

bottom face of top die = 2

top of second = 3
bottom of second = 4

top of third = 6
bottom of third = 1

top of fourth = 3
bottom of fourth = 4

Use a little showmanship; don't give the answer too quickly, and you can probably get away with this trick many times.

In this example, subtract five from 28 and the total of the seven hidden faces has to be 23.

Make several stacks of dice and check out this trick for yourself. Then amaze your friends with your skill.

Drop Shot

The trick that makes this stunt work is making sure your opponent goes first.

Place a saucepan or kettle on the floor. Or, if you prefer, turn a hat or cap upside down on the floor.

Take ten cards from a deck. Make the following challenge.

"I will hand you these cards one at a time.

Hold the card at waist level above the pan. Drop it into the pan. You drop ten cards. Then I will drop ten. The one who gets the most cards into the pan wins."

That's all there is to it—a simple test of skill. (Naturally, there is a trick to it.)

When you hand your opponent the cards, make sure to hold the cards with an edge

pointing down. Most likely your friend will drop the cards that way.

Drop a few cards by one edge and see what happens as they fall.

Now hold a card *flat*. Hold it by two edges and let go of it so that it falls with the flat side parallel to the floor.

Do it a few times and you'll see the difference. Cards dropped like that are more likely to fall nearly straight down. Cards dropped with an edge down tend to flutter off to one side before reaching the floor.

If your opponent always goes first, you should win this contest without any problems.

The Standing Card

A playing card or any three-by-five file card can be made to stand on edge. All it takes is a little know-how.

Pretend to work hard at making the card stand on edge—any edge. Of course, it keeps falling over.

Insist that you saw someone do this trick.

"I won't give up until I make this card stand," you say.

Just as soon as anyone tells you that this trick is impossible to do, you have the signal to perform.

Hold the card in the palm of one hand. Cup your fingers just slightly. This puts a curve into the card. Press the curve into the card with the fingers of your other hand. Within a few seconds the card will have the same slight curve itself. It won't be flat anymore.

Now stand the card with one of the curved edges on the table. It will stand up just the way you said it would.

"There. I knew it would stand by itself!" you announce.

Don't expect people to congratulate you. It's hard to say nice things when you're grinding your teeth!

The Next Card Is Yours

Just about everyone enjoys being asked to pick a card from a pack and then trying to hide it so that it cannot be identified. This is one time when the victim may enjoy the trick even more than you do.

For this stunt, you need a deck of cards with a picture on the back. *Don't* use cards with a back design that looks the same upside down or right side up. A picture of a dog or boat (or anything that's different when turned around) is what you need.

Before showing this trick to anyone, go through the deck and make sure all the backs are turned the same way. Hold the deck out to your victim. You may want to fan the cards when you do this.

You say, "Pick one card. Do not let go of it. Memorize that card."

While the victim is intent upon that one

card, turn the deck in your hand. If you turn the deck casually, your victim will never notice.

"Slip the card into the deck," you say, continuing the trick.

(By now, the trick is already obvious to you. All the cards are now pointing one way *except* for the chosen card.) Cut the deck three or four times to conceal the chosen card. Be absolutely certain you don't turn any part of the deck as you do that.

"Now to locate your card," you can say confidently.

Leave the deck with the backs of the cards facing up. Slowly turn over the cards, one at a time. The chosen card will be easy to spot. It will be the one whose back faces the wrong way.

Don't react until you see the card's face, of course. When this card's face appears you can make a little production out of it.

"Is this the one?" Hesitate and look

puzzled. You may even start to turn over another card. Then go back, shake your head and say, "This is the one, isn't it?"

If you repeat this trick, naturally, you must turn the card so that it again points in the same direction as the rest of the deck.

If you want to be really tricky about this, here's an idea: When you locate the proper card, memorize its face, but don't say anything. Instead, continue turning over a few more cards. Then begin to look bothered. Turn over one more card. Smile and look pleased.

"The next card I pick up is your card," you can tell your victim.

No way! The chosen card was turned up several cards back. Your victim is pretty certain you've tricked yourself and will probably say something like, "I'll bet you are wrong."

After your victim lets you know how

wrong you are, go back through the cards and pick up the right one. Then watch your victim, who has just been tricked—but good!

The Tattletale Reversed Card

When you want to really confuse others with your trickery, show them this card trick.
Place five or six cards on the table. Build up to your trick like this.

Say, "In just a minute, I am going to turn my back. While my back is turned, I want you to reverse one of these cards. Put it

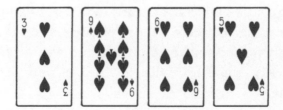

back in its exact place. Then I will turn around and be able to tell you which card you reversed."

Naturally, you can do exactly what you claim to do. Study the cards shown to see how this trick works.

Take a good look at the three of hearts; two of the hearts point downward and only one points upward. The nine of spades has five spades pointing upward and only four pointing downward. The same is true for the six of hearts and five of hearts.

Can you now see how the trick works? When one of these cards is reversed, there will be a difference in the way the spots or markings appear to you. Reverse the three of hearts, and suddenly two hearts point upward instead of downward.

Flip through a deck of cards. You will find a number of cards that are different when they are reversed. Choose five or six of these different cards and get ready to show your trick.

Beware of sevens and aces! Sevens and aces (except for the ace of diamonds) can be used for this trick, but they are too obvious and would give the trick away. Take a look at them yourself to see why.

You may want to add a little hocus-pocus with this trick. "Cards have a way of telling people they have been touched," you may tell the person you want to trick. "They give off heat from your hand. No matter how lightly you touch a card, just the contact changes that card. I can feel that when I run my hand over the cards."

This is utter nonsense and most people know it. Some victims will touch all the cards in an effort to throw you off, however.

After a card is reversed, you can tell at a glance which one was turned. In the above illustration, all four cards have the greatest number of one-way markings at the top of the card. It's simple to identify the one that is reversed.

To really convince people how tricky you can be, allow your victim to reverse more than one card or even not to reverse any cards.

"I will know. The cards always tell me," you can boast—which is true, isn't it?

The Tattletale Chosen Card

Once you have The Tattletale Reversed Card stunt under control, try this one.

Sort through a deck of cards and pull out *all* the cards that change their appearance when they are reversed. This includes the sevens and aces, as well as most threes, fives, sixes, and nines.

If some tricky person asks why there aren't any diamonds, you can show the seven and, hopefully, end the questions. Or you can say, "I don't like red diamonds. They make me think of stop signs and that sort of thing." You can come up with some good reason.

Set up the cards you have chosen so that they all "point" in the same direction, like this example.

"Pick a card," you instruct your opponent. "Memorize it."

While the other person's attention is on the card just picked, you reverse the deck (like the trick "The Next Card Is Yours").

When the chosen card is slipped back into the deck, it will "point" in the opposite direction from the others in the pack.

Make a show of turning the cards face up, one at a time. It won't be hard to spot the chosen card. Pull it out and hand it over. As you do, it's the most natural thing in the world to give it a half turn while you offer it to the other person. This, of course, has it "pointing" the same way as the other cards. Just make sure it stays this way when it's returned to the pack.

This trick borrows ideas from two other tricks but comes out with an entirely new version. It illustrates how really clever you can become when learning the game.

Mind-Reading Dice

Hand your victim any three dice and say something like this:

"If you can do some fourth-grade math, I can make these dice into mind-reading dice. You can even use a calculator."

Naturally, your victim can do fourth-grade math. What sort of question is that?

"Just to prove I can do a mind-reading trick with these dice I want you to roll them. Be sure to keep them out of my sight. But this is very important. Don't touch them after they stop rolling. If you touch them you'll ruin the trick."

This is all nonsense. But the dice roller doesn't know that. The warning about not touching the dice is what is called "misdirection." It makes your victim wonder what would happen if the dice were touched, instead of thinking about how the trick works.

Once the dice are rolled, and with your back still turned, give these instructions:

"Double the number of spots showing on the die that is farthest to your left.

"Now, add five to the number you got when you doubled.

"Multiply this answer by five.

"Now, add the number of spots showing on the middle die.

"Next, multiply that last answer by ten.

"Add to this last answer the number of spots on the third die.

"Finally, tell me the total you got when you added the final number."

Once you have that total number, you pretend to concentrate hard for a few seconds. Then look pleased, and tell your victim the number of spots showing on each of the three dice.

This is a good stunt, which works over and over. The only way it can go wrong is if one of you messes up the math.

Double the spots on the left-hand die: $5 \times 2 = 10$.

Add five: $10 + 5 = 15$.

Multiply by five: $15 \times 5 = 75$.

Add the middle die: $75 + 6 = 81$.

Multiply by ten: $81 \times 10 = 810$.

Add three: $810 + 3 = 813$.

Now, without telling your victim what you are doing, you must subtract 250 from the answer: $813 - 250 = 563$. The answer you got, 563, gives you the top numbers of the three dice in order from left to right—without fail.

The Last Card

When people are showing off their best card tricks, you may want to demonstrate this sneaky little fooler.

"What I am going to do," you tell your friends, "is to name the last card one of you turns over."

Give this trick all the buildup you want. Shuffle the deck a few times. Then give it to your victim and suggest, "Why don't you shuffle the deck yourself?"

Then you say, "Please cut the deck at least four times."

Once this is all taken care of, ask for part of the deck of cards. "Cut the deck one more time," you'll say, "Without looking at any of the cards, give half of the deck to me. You take the other half."

When you have your cards in hand, say, "Now, go into the next room. Close the door behind you. Turn over as many cards from your part of the deck as you want. After you have turned over some or even all the cards, come back into this room. When you do I'll tell you the card that was the last one you turned over."

Who can resist the chance to prove you can't do what you say?

As soon as your friend walks into the next room and the door closes, take one card from your part of the pack. Lean that card against the closed door. When the door opens, this card will get turned over.

Naturally, you can name the last card to be turned over. After all, you chose it.

You Picked This Card?

People are quite used to being asked to pick a card from a deck. The trick is always that the magician, or trickster, will then discover that one particular card.

This trick is really annoying.

Tell your victim, "Pick a card. Any card. Don't let me see it. Memorize it. Put it back into the pack. Then shuffle the pack. Cut it as many times as you wish."

When this is done, ask for the cards. Announce, "I will hand you the card you picked."

All you have to do is return the cards to your victim.

"Here. The card you picked is in here. I just handed you the card you picked."

You can expect some nasty remarks when the victim realizes you have played one more trick. If those things bothered you,

you wouldn't be playing more sneaky tricks.

If you want to make this trick last longer, hand your victim one card at a time. Each time, ask, "Is this the card?"

You will eventually reach the correct card. When that happens, you might look pleased with yourself and say, "See, I told you I'd hand you the card you picked."

Don't expect much praise, especially if you went through most of the deck to reach the chosen card.

TRICKS WITH STRINGS AND THINGS

Don't Lose Your Head

Start with a piece of string about three feet long; tie the two ends together.

Drape the string around your neck with both ends hanging in front of you in two loops. Put one thumb through each of the loops and pull the string tight (not tight enough to strangle yourself—that would ruin the trick).

Move your hands close together. As you do so, extend the index finger (pointer) of one hand. With this index finger reach over and hook the loop held by the other hand. Keep the string tight all this time.

(For this example, if you have used the right index finger, that right finger is now sharing the loop with your left thumb.)

At this point, say something stunning, such as, "I am going to pull this string through my neck." Or, to be more dramatic you can say, "I'm going to cut off my head."

As you say this, slip your *right* thumb out of the loop. At the same moment, quickly pull your right index finger and your left thumb in opposite directions. Be sure to keep the string tight.

Almost by magic, the string seems to slice through your neck! Of course, it just slides *around* your neck as your right index finger and left thumb separate.

Magicians call this trick an illusion. Most people call it sneaky. No matter what you call it, this one always surprises people the first time they see it.

Tying a Tricky Knot

For this trick, you need a piece of string about three feet long. You can also use a scarf or a large handkerchief instead of the string.

Hold up the string, or whatever, so that one end is in your right hand and the other is in your left.

Announce, "I can tie a knot in this piece of string."

That's not exactly the news story of the year, but it will let your victims know you have another trick for them.

"I can tie a knot in this string *without* letting go of either end."

This boast is something else! It's clearly impossible. Or is it?

Let your audience experiment before you begin. If someone else knows the trick, you can compliment that person and say, "See, I told you it could be done."

But if everyone else fails you can come to the rescue. Just fold your arms. Then take hold of one end of the string in each hand. (It is trickier to get hold of the two ends with your arms folded than it is to do the trick!)

To tie the knot, just unfold your arms while holding onto the ends of the cord. A knot will appear in the middle of the cord.

Your victims will undoubtedly say, "Oh, that's easy."

Just remind them it was you who showed them how.

A Knotty Problem

Tying a knot in the middle of a shoelace or piece of cord is not much of a trick. But tying a knot using only one hand makes it much more interesting.

Hold a fairly long shoelace or piece of cord in your hand. Work up to this trick with a few well-chosen words, such as:

"When you are as skillful and as talented as I am, it's easy to do things other people find nearly impossible."

After an opening like that who can resist taking a potshot at you?

You continue, "Just using one hand I can tie a knot in this shoelace. I won't let the lace touch the rest of my body. I won't have to cheat by letting the lace touch anything besides my hand."

Your victim will take a look at the lace and decide the task can't be all that difficult. After all, you say you can do it. Why can't anyone?

It is not impossible to tie the necessary knot. It is just difficult—unless you do it properly. That, of course, is the trick.

Let your victims work on this trick for a few minutes. Don't be surprised if someone manages to get a knot into the lace. It can be done. Just don't allow the lace to touch anything but the player's hand and fingers.

If someone gets the knot into place, be quick to congratulate that person. Then add, "Of course, I can do it in less than five seconds!" This is probably a lot quicker than the time it takes anyone else to tie the knot.

When the time comes to put up or shut up, be ready to amaze and dazzle. If you practice this trick a few times, you'll be able to do it quickly enough so that the people watching *still* won't be able to tie the knot, even though they just saw it done!

Hang the shoelace or cord over your thumb as shown below. Let the end next to your palm hang down lower than the other end.

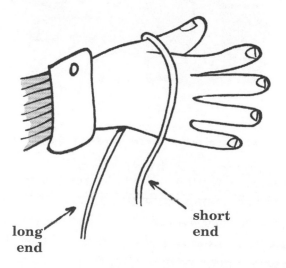

long end

short end

First, hook the long side of the cord with your ring finger so that it is now tucked between your middle finger and your ring finger. (See top of page 194).

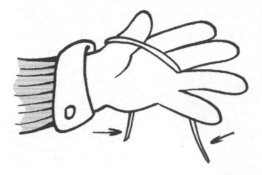

Next, turn your hand so that your palm is now facing the floor. As you turn your hand palm down, tilt you hand so the short end of the cord swings forward and across the cord between the tip of your thumb and forefinger. It should cross in front of the string tucked under your middle finger.

Then tip your hand downward. The loop on the back of your hand will slide off your fingers. Hold tightly onto the short end of the cord and jerk your hand upward.

Believe it or not, that's all there is to it. There you are, holding the end of the cord between your thumb and forefinger. A knot has been made somewhere down on the shoelace or cord.

Though it may be difficult, try to look modest as you show your victims how quickly you tied the knot using only your wits and one hand.

The Famous Ring-Off-the-String Trick

This trick is not magic, though many magicians use it to amaze their audiences. It is absolutely, positively, *guaranteed* to surprise your victim. You'll need string and a ring.

Begin with a piece of string about three feet long. Tie the ends together. Now you have a loop of string. Have your victim (or helper, or whoever) hold up both index fingers.

Slip one end of the loop over one index finger. Run the rest of the string through the middle of the ring you brought. Loop the other end of the string over your friend's other index finger.

"Now," you announce, "here is what I am going to do. I am going to remove the ring from the string. The string won't be cut or untied. Neither will it be slipped from either index finger."

It doesn't take a whole lot of thinking to realize that this seems impossible. Of course it is not. Otherwise, how could you make this trick work?

Facing your helper, with your left hand take hold of the side of the string that's farther from you. Pull it *over* the nearer part of the string and hold onto it.

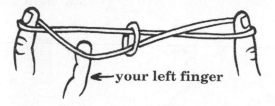

←your left finger

Next, reach *under* the part of the string you are holding with your left hand. Take hold of the far string. Pull it toward you. Make certain the ring is to your right and out of the way.

As you pull on the string with your right hand you will form a loop. The person holding the string will have to move both hands a little closer together to give you the slack you need to make the loop.

Hook this loop over the holder's right finger. Since you are facing the person holding the string, this is the finger to *your left*.

Once this loop is hooked over the holder's

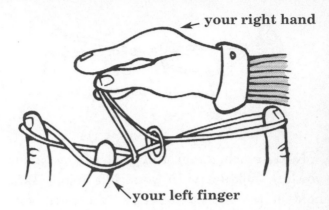

← your right hand

← your left finger

index finger let go of it with your right hand. *Do not* let go of the string your left hand is still holding.

Now it is time to work to *your right* of the ring. Reach over the string nearer to you. Take hold of the farther string with your right hand. Don't let go with your left hand or you'll have to start all over again.

With your right hand, gently pull one more loop in the string. Your holder will have to let you have enough string to work with by moving both hands closer together again.

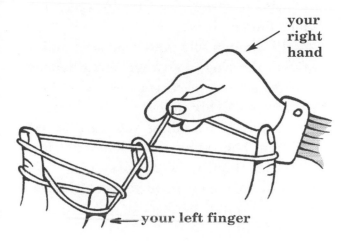

your right hand

←— your left finger

Now, for the moment of truth! Take hold of the ring with your right hand. Let go of the loop of string you have held for so long with your left hand.

Maybe you want to say, "Brace yourself," to the string holder. Then very, very slowly begin to pull on the ring. You may need to wiggle the ring up and down a bit because those loops of string need to slip around the holder's finger.

As the strings slip and you keep pulling gently on the ring, a strange thing happens. To everyone's surprise (maybe even yours) the ring is suddenly pulled off the string.

There you are holding the ring in your right hand. The string never left the holder's fingers—yet the ring is off the string!

Practice this one until you get the technique smooth and perfect. It will help build your reputation as a really tricky character.

Tricky Ice Cube Pickup

It is not difficult to pick up an ice cube. Most of us do it every day. If you tell someone you can pick up an ice cube, the best you can expect is a laugh or a shake of the head.

But tell that same person you can pick up an ice cube with a short piece of string and you'll see some interest.

"I can pick up an ice cube with this piece of string. I won't touch the ice cube with my fingers in any way. All I have to do is to place my tricky string in my hand, and the string will lift the ice cube," you can predict.

Your victim will probably demand to see this tricky piece of string. Since the string is really just a common ordinary piece of string, there is nothing to see.

Offer to let your victim use your tricky string.

"What if I tie a loop in this string?" he or she may ask first.

"I don't have to tie a loop in the string," you reply. "Anyone can do it that way."

Eventually, most people will give up after trying to pick up the melting ice cube without success. A lucky individual may manage to wind the string around the cube and lift it, but this is a clumsy way of doing things.

When it is time for you to show your stuff, get a fresh ice cube from the freezer. Wet the end of your string. Drop the wet end onto the ice cube. Sprinkle a bit of salt onto the wet end of the string and the surrounding ice.

Wait a few seconds; then gently lift the string. The ice cube should come right up. Just to be on the safe side, practice this a couple of times before you perform this trick. You don't have to use a fresh ice cube, but since the one from the freezer will be colder than the one your victim has been messing with, it works better.

Modern Matches

In the days when people used wooden matches to light stoves and fireplaces, puzzlers like this one were called "matchstick problems." Toothpicks make more modern markers or, when they're not handy, pencil and paper and a good eraser will do the job.

The object in brain teasers of this sort is to change one figure to a new shape by moving or removing one or more matches, toothpicks, or lines. We'll begin with a simple one to get you going.

Let's say you set up the figure below with toothpicks. This is the dare. Take away only

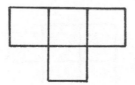

one toothpick to make a figure that contains only three squares.

As you do these puzzles and later when you dare others to do them, keep one thing in mind. A square has *four* sides equal in length. (A rectangle may have two short and two long sides.) Don't try to claim an answer that does not have squares but has rectangles instead. And don't leave a line hanging in space. Every solution must form perfect squares. No loose lines are allowed!

Once you ace that, here's a second problem. Starting with a new shape but the same rules, take away six sides so that only two squares are left. Here's a hint: Squares come in many sizes.

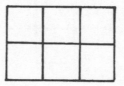

Now try to remove eight toothpicks from a different starting shape, to leave four squares behind.

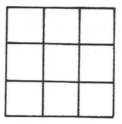

Next time, take away six toothpicks so that only three squares remain in the figure.

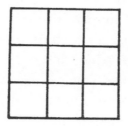

For a final puzzle, you will be moving sticks instead of taking them away from the figure. Move three toothpicks to new locations so your new figure will contain four squares.

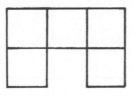

After checking your answers with the ones that are upside down you should be ready to present these puzzles to your friends. You might also take a crack at making up toothpick challenges of your own. The five you tried are only a few of the possible puzzles you can use to stump your friends. There are many more just waiting for you to find them.

Turn the page upside down for the answers.

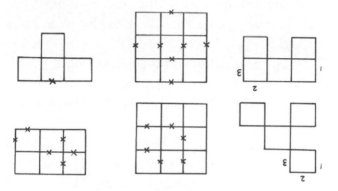

The side to be removed is marked with an X.

−207−

Magic Match

Can you make something move using your mind? Sure you can. All it takes is a little thought.

Snap a wooden toothpick in half. Don't break it into two pieces; be sure the toothpick is still held together by the fibers along one side.

Place the snapped toothpick carefully on the table in front of your future victim. Say, "I bet I can make this toothpick move. I won't hit the table. I won't blow on the toothpick. I won't push it with a stick or any such thing. But in spite of the fact that I won't touch the toothpick or the table, I can make that pick move."

After your victim has asked you about a number of possible tricks that you deny, your dare will probably be accepted.

Use a spoon, your fingers, or a pop-top

sports bottle to carry a drop of water to the table. Release just one drop of water onto the broken part of the toothpick. As the wood in the pick swells from the water, the toothpick will begin to open slightly. The broken spot acts as a hinge.

Try it on your own just to prove to yourself that this trick really works.

Standing Room Only

If you tell someone you can balance a wooden matchstick on a plate or dish it doesn't sound like much of a trick. When your victim yawns or seems unimpressed it's time for action. (A *used* match is safest to use in any trick, so ask for some from an adult to practice and play this one.)

"Here you go," you might say. Hand this

person a used wooden match and a dish or saucer. "Why don't you make this match stand up on the dish?"

Give your unfortunate friend time enough to become really frustrated before showing how the trick works.

Whether you get pretty tricky or not yourself is entirely up to you. If you want to be tricky, hold the wooden end of the match between your lips (not the head of the match, naturally) as you pretend to position the dish just so.

What you are doing is getting the end of the match really damp. Once the end of the match is moistened, press it down hard onto the plate. Hold it in place for a few seconds while mashing it down good and hard.

Think of something confusing to say to cover the fact that you are pressing down so hard on the damp match fibers.

"Due to the earth's movement through

space I have to hold the match long enough for it to adjust to its changed position," is a possible statement.

Or you can say, "I am realigning the match's molecules."

When you let go of the match it *should* stand upright. If it topples, repeat all the moves and try again.

The best part of this trick is the reaction you get when people see you do what they couldn't do. Whether or not you want to conceal the fact that you dampened the end of the match is entirely up to you.

The Balancing Game

Stand a nickel on its side on top of a desk or tabletop. Then carefully balance a wooden toothpick on the top edge of the nickel. It doesn't matter whether the match is new or used.

Since this balancing act is a trick all its own, you may want to practice it a few times before performing the trick.

Now, place an empty glass upside down, over the coin and balanced toothpick. Be careful not to hit the end of the pick or your trick is over before you start. Make sure the glass is large enough so that the ends of the pick don't touch the sides of the glass.

"Now," you say, "here is what I dare you to do. I challenge you to make the toothpick fall off the top of the nickel. But the nickel must not fall over.

"You may not hit the table. You may not move the glass or hit it. It is not necessary to touch the table at all."

It won't take long before everyone decides this is impossible. (Everyone, that is, except you.) Let your victims puzzle over this one before showing them the trick.

All it takes is a comb made of hard rubber or some kind of plastic.

Run the comb through your hair a few times. This builds up a charge of static

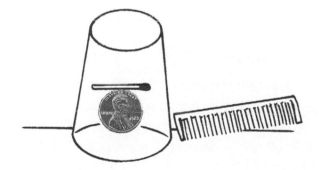

electricity on the comb's surface. Hold one end of the comb near the end of the toothpick and slowly move it. If you have enough static electricity built up, the match will begin to turn. As it turns, it will fall off the edge of the nickel. That's all there is to it.

Before performing this trick, practice it a few times. Unfortunately, some combs won't work; find one that does. And if your hair is very short, get your trick's victims to volunteer their hair for combing!

Hanging by a Thread

To get the attention of your victim, take a piece of string a couple of feet long and tie one end of it around a pen or pencil. Tie the other end of the string into a loop and let your friend hold it. Now, you're ready for action.

"I bet I can cut the string you are holding

and leave the pen hanging in air," you claim. Go on to add, "I won't even try to catch it after I cut the string. I'll cut the string about halfway between the pen and your hand. After I cut the string, I won't touch that pencil."

This will be too much for your friend to believe. It is time to prove you're a genius—or at least a brilliant prankster.

First, tie a knot to form a loop in the middle of the string. Now, simply cut the string in the middle of the loop.

The pen or pencil will not fall. You'll have won! And your victim will go in search of another victim as a chain of challenges is born.

Magic Yardstick

Here's a stunt that's all about mind over matter...or muscles. You'll need a yardstick for this trick.

Stick out your index fingers and place the yardstick across them so that one index finger rests under each end of the yardstick. Then

very slowly begin to move your fingers toward each other. First one finger will move and then the other. They won't always move at the same time but both fingers will eventually shift to meet in the middle of the yardstick. Remember! Move your fingers slowly with this stunt.

Once your fingers are together near the middle of the yardstick, begin slowly moving them apart. Surprise! One finger moves and the other stays right about where it was.

Regardless of how many times you repeat this prank, the same thing will always happen. When coming together, your fingers meet in the middle. When pulling apart from the center, one finger moves while the other stays in place.

You'll need to try this one a few times before you believe it. Then let others try it. So long as the fingers are moved slowly you can bet on the outcome and always be the same.

WORD PLAY

Spelling Lesson

Word tricks are easy to play on people any time, any place. Here's one that might stump even you at first, so don't peek at the answer below. Study this jumble of letters:

A D O O N Y E R W O O E N D N L N

Move them so they spell one word and only one.

Don't worry about words you have never heard of. Don't bother trying to think of people's names, foreign countries, or other strange and wonderful words and names.

Just stick to common words and you'll do fine.

If you get stuck, and many do, the answer is upside down on this page.

Whether you have to check the answer or find it on your own, this is a good word trick to use on the person who is a whiz at spelling and who never makes a mistake.

Turn the page upside down for the answer.

Sort the letters so they spell ONE WORD AND ONLY ONE.

How Many T's?

Give this quick trick a good buildup. Tell your victims something to make them curious. "It's amazing how few people can listen to even a sentence or two. They think they're listening, but really are not. I guess some people just aren't as smart as they think they are."

Naturally, your victims will want to show that they can listen. Everyone will be ready to demonstrate intelligence.

Once you have your victims practically begging to take part in your listening test, the rest is easy.

"Listen closely to what I say," you instruct.

Then, slowly and carefully, you say: "Tommy Tucker talks too much. His teacher should tell him to stop. Now tell me how many Ts there are in that."

If your victims ask you to repeat the

statement, do so. *Repeat it exactly as it is written on page 221.* Speak slowly and clearly. Make certain you pronounce each word carefully. Give your listeners all the time they need.

You may be surprised at the answers you receive. It is true that many people don't really listen. It's also true that most people find it difficult to count the number of letters that appear in a statement.

Of course, the correct answer is two. There are two T's in the word "that." That's what you asked. Quite clearly you said, "Now tell me how many T's there are in that."

Wrong-Answer Time

Lots of tricks work because the person playing the trick knows exactly what to say and when to say it. By saying the right thing at the right time, it is usually possible to keep your victim off guard. That is how this trick works.

You say, "Did you know that it is almost impossible to deliberately give wrong answers to questions?" (This is a good way to begin.)

"In fact," you'll continue, "I just heard that a person's mind will never deliberately give five wrong answers in a row."

This statement is more than most people can accept. When someone says, "I can give five wrong answers," you have a victim. The rest is up to you.

Begin by asking, "What year were you born?"

"In 1266," is a possible (certainly incorrect) answer.

Next, you might ask, "How many ounces are in a pound?"

Your victim may reply, "90."

You could begin to look a bit worried, as though you are in trouble.

"What is the sum of six and seven?" you ask, continuing the game.

Expect a silly answer, such as "569."

Hesitate for a second or two. Then ask, "How many questions is that so far?"

Unless you victim is sharper than the average bear, he or she will answer, "Three." If that happens, you have won your bet.

Your victim may see through the trick and give you a wrong answer instead. When that happens you have to be your most tricky.

Grin, shrug and ask, "Oh, did I try this trick on you already?"

You may luck out and be told, "No, I just guessed it."

Of course, this answer is correct and you win. If you get another wild answer, you just struck out. Sorry about that!

That Can't Be a Word

This catchy little trick is a good one to try on a fantastic speller or someone who reads a lot.

Begin by claiming, "I know an eight-letter word. This word used to be important, but is not heard or written much anymore. Another hint, George Washington and Ben Franklin both used it. So did your great-grandmother."

By now, you can almost hear the mental wheels beginning to turn.

You continue, "In this word, the three letters K S T are in the middle; in the beginning; and at the end."

Your fantastic speller is really thinking now. What eight-letter word has K S T in the middle, in the beginning, and at the end?

If your victim realizes that this seems to add up to nine (instead of eight) letters, just flash your best evil smile. Obviously, there can't be such a word.

Most people give up pretty quickly.

"The word is INKSTAND," you announce to the quitter. "It has 'K S T' in the middle, 'IN' is the beginning. Of course, 'AND' is at the end."

IN KST AND

This is not exactly the way you described the word, but what you said was true enough. A little misdirection makes lots of tricks work. This is one of them.

Reading Lesson

Reading is one of the most important of all skills. This quick problem will test your skill in reading before you try it on other dupes. Just read the following proverb from Ben Franklin.

EARLY TO BED

AND EARLY TO

TO RISE MAKES

A MAN HEALTHY,

WEALTHY, AND WISE

Did you read the proverb exactly as it is written here? Read it again to make sure. Then, just to be on the safe side, check the upside-down answer.

This is an excellent little problem to present to others. Type Franklin's proverb on a card or piece of paper, or print it in block letters exactly as above. Ask your victim to read aloud exactly what is there. Most people will find they need a bit of help with their reading after they take your reading test.

Turn the page upside down for the answer.

Look at lines two and three. They read "EARLY TO TO RISE"—there is an extra "to" in the proverb.

Little Red Fire Truck

Here is a spoken puzzle that really makes people wonder whether or not they are losing their minds. Ask your victim to repeat exactly what you say. Then begin.

Say, "Little red fire truck."

Naturally, your pigeon says, "Little red fire truck."

Next say, "Little red, blue, red fire truck."

Most people will repeat, "Little red, blue, red fire truck." Grin, shake your head, and

say quickly, "See, I knew you couldn't do it!"

At that point your victim probably will look puzzled and ask for you to do it again. If he or she doesn't, you might suggest taking another crack at it.

Then, do as before.

Say, "Little red fire truck." Then say, "Little red, blue, red fire truck."

Then, as before, shake your head and say something like, "You messed up again!" or "You still haven't got it right!"

Of course, the trick is that your victim must repeat what you say every time, *including* the third time you speak. That means repeating "See, I knew you couldn't do it!" or "You messed up again!" or whatever it was you said.

It is amazing how many people you can trick time after time with this little puzzle.

The Joke's on Me

Don't you know someone who is just a little bit too smart? Here's your chance to bring that person down to size—or at least get a laugh.

Tell your victim you are going to spell a few words that you'd like to hear pronounced. Be sure the person understands that all he or she has to do is just say the word.

Begin by saying, "What does s-m-o-k-e spell?"

Of course, the answer is "smoke."

Now ask, "What does j-o-k-e spell?"

And, naturally, the answer will be "joke."

Now ask, "What does f-o-l-k spell?"

Your victim will tell you that spells "folk."

Then say, "What is the white of an egg?"

Unless your victim is a lot more careful than most people, the answer will be "yolk."

When that happens, it is time for you to look superior. You can say something like "Don't you know the yolk is the *yellow* part of the egg?" And, of course, the joke is on your victim.

If your victim is really as smart as you think, you might be told that the white of an egg is the albumen. If that happens, then the joke is on you for trying this stunt with an egghead!

Carrying Water in a Tissue

Set up this trick by pulling a facial tissue out of its box. Pretend to examine it very carefully.

"These tissues are really strong," you can say to begin."

Then, as though the thought just struck, you add, "I think I can carry water in this tissue. What do you think?"

Of course, your victim doesn't think it's possible. When a person pours or runs water into a facial tissue, the result is a soggy mess.

If your victim says it's impossible, offer to prove that it can be done. Should your victim think it is possible, ask him or her to show you how. Either way, you've got your trick going.

Since water is usually found in the kitchen, that's the place to go. To prove your point, take the tissue in one hand. Open the refrigerator's freezer door and take out an ice cube. Wrap the cube in the tissue and carry it across the room. It's as simple as that.

If your victim protests, ask, "What is ice?" The only possible answer is, "Frozen water."

If that's not good enough, hand the ice cube to your friend.

"Hold onto this for a few minutes. When it

starts to melt you'll have all the water your want."

That should be all it takes. You've won again.

Grandmother Does Not Like Tea

Before you are ready to go out and puzzle others with this listening game, it might be a good idea for you to figure out for yourself just what grandmother does and does not like.

Grandmother likes milk but does not like buttermilk.

She likes cheese but hates cottage cheese.

She loves spinach and does not like lettuce.

Grandmother is fond of celery but dislikes beets.

She goes for oranges but does not eat grapefruit.

Grandmother enjoys cabbage but dislikes turnips.

She is fond of her nephews but does not care for her brothers.

Grandmother likes her grandsons but detests her granddaughters.

She likes purple but dislikes violet.

Wednesday is fine but Thursday is terrible.

Grandmother enjoys July and dislikes August.

Are you ready to dream up some other pairs of things Grandmother does and does not like? First, just to be absolutely certain you are onto the game, check the upside-down answer on this page. Then go in search of listeners.

This listening puzzle is so simple yet often drives people crazy. This is especially so when three or four players in a group pick up on it at once but one or two remain in the dark.

Turn the page upside down for the answer.

Grandmother does not like any word or name with the letter T in it.

Look Sharp

Believe it or not, their are five errers in this short paragraph. Study the paragraph carefully. Feel free to reed it as many times as necessary. Don't give up to easily. Keep at it until you find all of them.

An answer is given below if you can't locate all five.

This is another of those great dares to present to the wise guy who knows everything. Just say, "I bet you can't find the five things wrong with this paragraph." Your victim can't help but accept a dare like that.

Turn the page upside down for the answer.

"There" is written as "their" and "errors" is spelled "errers," while "read" is written as "reed." The "to" in the fourth sentence should be "too." The fifth error, the hard one to spot, is that the paragraph only contains four errors, not five.

Think Fast!

It is surprising how many people get nervous when they are asked to do something simple in a certain amount of time. Faced with the time limit, lots of people do easy things quite poorly.

Tell victims that you're willing to bet they can't name ten parts of the body within thirty seconds. Before anyone begins to

rattle off names, be sure the victim under-stands the full dare.

"There are at least eleven body parts that are spelled using three letters and are not slang expressions," you should say. "I bet you can't name ten of them in thirty seconds. In fact, I'm so certain, I'll even give you the trickiest word—'fat'—to get you started. Ready, set, go. Hurry, because I'm timing you."

Try this one yourself. Can you name ten more three-letter body parts in half a minute? Bet you can't!

Turn the page upside down for the answer.

Leg; toe; hip; rib; arm; eye; ear; lip; gum; jaw.

Spelling Can Be Hard

Find an opponent who is a fairly good speller. Dare that person to spell three words correctly aloud, from a list of words you choose. Stress the fact that he or she may make only one attempt to spell each word.

Once the dare has been accepted, you are ready to begin.

Tell your victim, "Spell receive."

He or she will probably spell out,

"R e c e i v e."

"Now spell neighbor," you continue.

The answer will probably be,

"N e i g h b o r."

At this point you say in a firm voice, "Wrong."

Your friend will doubtless protest and say something to the effect,

"N e i g h b o r
spells neighbor."

Again you say, "Wrong."

This goes on and on until your victim either catches on to the fact he or she was supposed to spell "wrong" or until you finally let a very frustrated person in on the trick.

Or, you can pretend to be willing to let your victim try again and go through a second set of words. Naturally, after the second spelling you'll say, "Wrong." And the whole cycle begins again.

Ride the Bus

In city after city, all over the world, people ride buses. Maybe that's why this puzzle is so popular. Be ready to answer a question when you finish reading the next paragraph.

Fred started his bus route yesterday morning by stopping at Hill Street where five

people got onto Fred's bus. When Fred stopped at Center Street, nine more people got onto the bus. At the Main Street stop, four people got on but six people got off Fred's bus. When Fred stopped at Lincoln Avenue, two people left the bus and only one woman got onto the bus. At the Grant Avenue stop two people got on and four got off. When

Fred stopped at Washington Place, six people were waiting to get on and three wanted to get off.

Now for the question: How many stops did the bus make in the paragraph you just read?

If you knew the answer without looking back you are much cleverer than most people. Generally, after the first few sentences, people suspect they will be asked how many passengers are on the bus or how many got off. Listeners get distracted trying to count passengers. Few people have any idea how many stops Fred's bus made.

Use this story or make up one like it to try on your friends. Tell it fairly quickly and say very clearly the numbers of people getting on and off. Then ask how many stops the bus made. You'll be able to catch a lot of listeners.

A Room for the Night

Before presenting this listening problem to your friends, it will be fun for you to read it through and try to solve it on your own.

Here's the way the story goes. Three fellows arrived at a bargain hotel. The clerk charged them $10 each for the night since they were all going to share one large room. After the clerk collected $30 he realized she should only have charged the men $25 for their room. He called for the bellhop and told him to take $5 back to the men.

The bellhop didn't know how to divide the $5 into three equal parts so he gave $1 each back to the men. The other $2 be kept for himself. The men got back $1 each. This meant they had each paid $9 for the room. Three men paying $9 each makes a total of $27 they paid for the room since three times nine is twenty-seven. The bellhop has $2.

Twenty-seven plus two equals twenty-nine. What happened to the missing dollar?

Work on this until you know what happened to the other dollar. Check the solution and then go looking for some friends you wish to confuse when you tell them, "I bet you can't tell me what's wrong with this little story."

Turn page upside down for answer.

The money is all there. The clerk still has $25. The bellhop has $2 and the men in the room have $3. It is all in the way the problem is stated. Looking at it another way, the men have now paid $27 for the room. Of that amount the clerk has $25 and the bellhop has $2.

Shoot for the Moon

Be certain you know how this listening game plays out before you try it on your friends.

The game's object is easy enough. Each player makes a statement in which two closely related things are named. There's a pattern that links all the things in the groups of "likes" and "dislikes"—but what is it?

For example, "I like to shoot but don't want to go hunting."

The moon is great but Neptune isn't all that hot.

Scissors are fine for cutting but a knife isn't.

Butter is good but margarine is lacking in taste.

Coffee is great but hot chocolate isn't my favorite.

Books are fun to read but magazines bore me.

Doors are important but windows are silly.

Fools are fun but clowns are a waste of my time.

School is the place to be because it is more fun than being at home.

I'd rather live in a village than in a town.

Deer are pretty animals but elk are too large.

Once you get the drift, you should be able to shoot for some pairs of your own. If you're still in doubt, consider this: Everything you "like" contains double letters. Get it? Then go looking for others who think they are pretty good listeners. This stunt stumps even the sharpest people for awhile.

Beauty without Brains

The easiest tricks often catch the most people. This one should do just that.

Dare someone by saying, "I bet you can't say beauty without brains three times."

Chances are your victim will say, "Beauty without brains, beauty without brains, beauty without brains."

At that point you smile and declare yourself the winner of the bet.

"I told you to say beauty without brains," you repeat. "Three times."

At which your victim will probably say again, "Beauty without brains, beauty without brains, beauty without brains."

And, once more, you can tell your opponent that you won.

Some people see through the trick and finally say, "Beauty, beauty, beauty." Some people never figure this one out and continue to repeat the error...again and again.

Say What?

All spoken dares depend upon how well you play your part. This is no exception.

Tell your victim you can get anyone to say the word "black."

If your dare is accepted, remember to set the ground rule that each question you ask must be answered. Once this is agreed on, you're ready to do your stuff.

You might go about it something like this:

"What is the opposite of white?"

Your opponent will give some answer that is not black, of course.

"What is the darkest color?"

You'll get another non-black answer.

"What is the color of a truck tire?"

Still another reply that is not black.

"What color is a bowling ball?"

Yet another answer, but not black.

"What color is a tar highway?"

You won't hear black in the answer.

Continue for another few questions and answers. Immediately after getting one of the non-black answers, let your face light up. Smile, look pleased, and tell your opponent. "You lose! I told you I'd get you to say_____." Insert whatever the person's last answer was. For example, if their last answer was "red" you'd say, "I told you I'd get you to say 'red.' You lose."

At this point most people will protest by saying something such as this: "You said I'd say 'black.'"

However they phrase it, your opponents will almost always fall for this trick by including the word "black" in their argument.

Of course you don't have to use "black" as the forbidden word. Any color, a number, or a person's name—whatever—will work just as well.

PSYCHIC TRICKS

Tricky Dice Totals

As you begin this trick, take a minute to tell your friends how you just happened to learn you had magic powers. Quite by accident, you discovered you could read the minds of people who rolled dice.

Naturally, no one will believe you. All you can do when that happens is to prove they're wrong.

Have someone roll two dice-without letting you see the numbers rolled.

You say: "Add the two numbers that are showing on top. Remember that total, but don't tell me."

Once this is done, tell your chosen stooge to pick up one of the dice, leaving the other where it landed.

"Read the number on the bottom and add it to the total you just got," you continue.

"Roll the same die you picked up," you'll go on. "Add the number that comes up on top to the total so far. Think very hard about that final amount. Do not touch either of the dice again."

When your helper has this final total in mind, it is time for you to take a look at the two dice. You glance at them and instantly tell anyone who is interested what the total number is that your helper has in mind. But you never saw either side of one die's first throw!

This trick seems so easy that it really frustrates people who see it. Time and time again, you have the proper total yet no one can see how you do it—which, of course, is what makes it such a great trick.

Here is how it works: When you look at the two dice, you see the original number on one of them. The other has the number from its second roll showing.

Quickly add those two numbers together in your head. Add seven to that number. The result is the total your helper has in mind. This trick works because you know the opposite sides of a die *always* equal seven when added together. You didn't have to see the two sides from the first throw; you already know that together they added up to seven.

Let's do a quick example: The dice are rolled. One shows three, the other shows five: 3 + 5 = 8.

Your helper picks up the three and see that there's four on the reverse side. Four added to eight brings the total to 12.

That die is rolled again and comes up two.

Add two to the sum so far: 2 + 12 = 14. This is the grand total.

When you glance at the dice you see the original throw's five on one die and the second throw's two. You add five and two to get seven. Then you add seven more and arrive at 14. Neat trick, did I hear you say?

Run through this with dice a few times before you do it in public. Just be sure you choose a helper—your victim—who can add. If that person makes mistakes in addition, your trick will go sour. You won't have to read minds to know what people think when your trick backfires!

With Both Eyes Open

Here's a little trick that will work for you more times than not.

Begin by telling your listeners that you have certain psychic powers. Say that you have found that you have the power to cause other people to open their eyes without ever touching them. Stress that you are able to do this simply by speaking certain magic words to them when they have their eyes closed.

"I bet I can do this to you," you dare.

Once your bet has been accepted, it's all up to you.

Mutter a few mysterious words and phrases while looking your partner in the eye. Then say, "Now, close your eyes."

The instant your opponent's eyes close, command sharply, "No, not that way. You did it all wrong!"

At this point most people automatically open their eyes in order to find out what they did wrong. When they do, you've won your bet.

What if they don't fall for your trick and keep their eyes closed? Then you've just lost a bet. Win a few—lose a few.

Mind Bender

You might like to set the stage for this stunt by telling a friend you have discovered how to read minds. Your friend probably won't believe this. When that happens, you are ready to prove your point.

Tell your friend—really your victim—to hold some coins in both hands. In one hand there should be odd number of coins and in the other hand an even number of coins. (Pebbles or scraps of paper will work just as well as coins.)

Be sure your friend does not tell you how many coins are hidden in each hand or which holds evens or odds. Once your friend has an even number of coins in one hand and an odd number of coins in the other, request a little arithmetic.

Have your friend silently multiply the number of coins in the right hand by two, then to multiply the number of coins in the left hand by three, then add the two totals together. Ask to be told their sum.

At this point, you can tell your friend you did some mind reading during the multiplying. If the sum you were given is an *even* number, predict that your friend is holding an even number of coins in the left hand. When you are given an *odd* number as the sum, say that the right hand holds an even number of coins.

The reason this stunt always works is because it is has to work correctly is based on the math principle that an even number multiplied by an even number results in an even product. An odd number times an even also produces an even. Only an odd number times an odd number has an odd number for its sum. Therefore, an odd number from your friend indicates an odd number of coins in the left hand, the side you asked to be multiplied by three.

Guess Again

Start a discussion of ESP and psychic abilities. Eventually, someone will suggest trying to find someone in the group with such abilities. If no one makes the suggestion, you do it. Without a "psychic," there is no trick.

Suggest that someone leave the group and go into another room. Tell the group to decide on one object. Everyone will think about that object. When the person returns to the room he or she will try to pick up thought waves and name the object.

Of course, it's just luck if the chosen object is named quickly. (Just luck, that is, unless someone *does* have psychic ability!)

Let two or three people try their luck with this game. Then send your selected victim out for a turn. Now, for the trick. Actually this is a reverse trick, as you will soon see.

Tell the others, "Let's make this person think he or she really has the power to read minds. No matter what the first guess is, we'll all look surprised and say that's what we were thinking about."

Naturally, the victim is surprised and pleased. Suggest a second attempt.

This time, tell the group it will be the second thing named.

The next time, make it the third thing named. Then go back to saying it is the first guess the victim makes.

By picking the second or third guess, victims don't catch on that they are being taken for a ride.

If the victim is a nice person you might eventually explain the trick. If not, you may decide not to, then when your victim brags about this newly discovered ability to others and is asked for a demonstration, the trick will be twice as good!

The Never-Wrong Mind Reader

"I learned to read minds," you can begin. Before anyone tells you this is impossible, hurry on. "It was in a book. I read how to do it."

For effect you might pause and then admit, "Of course, I haven't tried it yet. But I know I can do it."

When your friends stop teasing you, it's time to do your thing. Hand a pencil and paper to one person.

"Here. Write any short message on that paper. Just don't let me see what it is."

Your victim will make sure you can't see what is being written while you pretend to think deep thoughts.

"Now fold the paper. I don't want anyone to think I saw what's on the paper," you say when the message is written.

Once the paper is folded, suggest, "Fold it again. I know I can tell what's on the paper."

When the second fold is finished, make your final request. "Just to be absolutely certain I can't see through the paper, put it on the floor. Then put your foot over it. That way there can't be any doubt."

By now, your victim is certain you've flipped your lid. Anyone who's watching is beginning either to suspect a trick or to wonder if you've lost your mind. Continue and say this with confidence:

"Now. Do you want me to tell you what is on the paper?"

(Notice that you never mention what is *written* on the paper? You always talk about what is *on* the paper.)

Of course, everyone wants to know what is *on* the paper.

"Your foot is on the paper. That's what's on the paper," you declare firmly.

You are right, of course. You have come through again, just like the winner you are!

Falling in Love Is Tricky

Start this number trick by using a little of your best showmanship. Say something like this, "I just discovered some magic numbers that tell me how many times you have been in love. To help me prove this, all you have to do is to follow my easy directions. The magic numbers will do the rest."

This is too good to turn down since most people are anxious to prove there are no such things as "magic numbers."

"Start by writing your age on a piece of paper," you direct.

"Now, multiply your age by two."

"Add five to the answer you got when you multiplied," you say next.

"Now multiply that answer by 50."

When your victim has done the multiplication you say, "Subtract the number of days in a normal year from the answer you just got." (That's 365, in case you run into someone who doesn't know.)

"Here's the most important step," you announce. "Add the number of times you have been in love. Since you're less than 100 years old, you can't have been in love more than 99 times, so don't try to fool me by saying you have!"

This direction is important for you. Any number *larger* than 99 in this step will mess up the magic answer.

When the addition is finished, you say, "Now add 115." Let your victim add the numbers. (Supply a calculator if you suspect your victim might have trouble with the math.)

Ask for the final answer. All it will take is a quick calculation for you to know your victim's age and also how many times he or she claims to have been in love.

Let's run through this for a person who's

12 years old and claims to have been in love
three times.

1.
$$\begin{array}{r} 12 \\ \times\ 2 \\ \hline 24 \end{array}$$

2.
$$\begin{array}{r} 24 \\ +\ 5 \\ \hline 29 \end{array}$$

3.
$$\begin{array}{r} 29 \\ \times\ 50 \\ \hline 1450 \end{array}$$

4.
$$\begin{array}{r} 1450 \\ +\ 365 \\ \hline 1085 \end{array}$$

5.
$$\begin{array}{r} 1085 \\ +\ 3 \\ \hline 1088 \end{array}$$

6.
$$\begin{array}{r} 1088 \\ +\ 115 \\ \hline 1203 \end{array}$$

age 12   03 or 3 times

When we look at the sum 1203 it's easy to see the first two digits tell the person's age is 12. The rest of the number indicates the number of times love has struck—three.

Work this problem through a few times for different ages and different numbers of times someone might have had a crush. The final amount can always be divided into two numbers: the age and times. If you don't let anyone claim to have been in love more than 99 times, this trick is a sure winner!

You Can Read My Mind

Instead of betting you can read someone else's mind, it's time to bet someone else can read yours.

Give this silly little stunt a bit of a build-up by saying you've discovered that it is sometimes possible to think very hard about a word or a phrase and cause others to be able to read your mind. After you've gotten the interest of the others, it is time to spring your trap.

"I'm willing to bet you can read my mind," you tell someone in the group. "Let's just see whether or not I'm right."

Then take a piece of paper and a pencil and turn your back on the person you have chosen. Carefully write a word on the paper. Fold the paper carefully two or three times, then turn back to the person you've dared to read your mind.

Ask, "Did you see what I just wrote on this paper?"

When the mind reader says, "No," it's really time for you to go into your act.

Act pleased, even delighted. Tell the mind reader how smart he or she is, and go on and on about it. Finally, unfold the paper and show everyone that you had indeed written "No" on the folded paper.

Obviously, your friend must have read your mind.

POTATOES, PAPER AND OTHER PROPS

Potato Pickup

Some tricks need tools but they're usually easy to find. A medium-sized potato and two plastic drinking straws are all you need for this quick trick.

A good way to begin is to say, "I can never figure out how people pick up their food with chopsticks. How could you pick up a potato with these?" By "these," you mean the plastic straws, of course.

After someone tells you it is impossible to pick up a whole potato with chopsticks or that straws are not chopsticks, it is time to set up your victims.

Insist that you saw someone pick up a potato with chopsticks made from drinking straws. "If he can do it, you should be able to," you may add.

Encourage your victims to at least make the attempt to do the trick. If your friends are determined enough, they will probably be able to lift the potato or apple between the ends of the straws by holding the straws right down at the bottom.

"That's the way." Compliment a job well done. Then say, "But now I remember. The person I saw did it with only one straw."

This is impossible and someone will tell you it is. But a good trickster never accepts defeat, and it's time for you to make your play.

Take the straw in your hand. Wrap your four fingers around it and place your thumb tightly over the open end at the top.

Make sure your thumb stays tightly over the opening. Plunge the straw down hard and fast into the potato or apple. It will stick into the potato without bending or breaking the straw.

Lift the potato by the straw and say, "I told you I could do it."

What happens is that your thumb traps

the air inside the straw. When you stab the potato, this trapped air compresses and keeps the straw straight.

Try this one before doing it in public. If you're having trouble, here's a tip: Apples are sometimes easier than potatoes to stab, so you can substitute the fruit for a potato.

Getting a Handle on It

This is a good follow-up stunt to use after you pick up a potato or an apple with a straw. In fact, you can use the same straw. You'll also need a bottle with a narrow neck.

(By the way, plastic bottles work best, especially the kinds with a "shoulder," such as the one shown on the following page. Beware of the large-sized soda bottles; they usually won't work.)

Waving the straw like a pointer, touch the

bottle with it. "I can pick up that bottle with this straw. And I won't even touch the bottle with my hands. All I'll do is hold onto the straw," you announce.

Let the others give it a try. The plastic straw isn't strong enough to lift the bottle, even if the bottle could be balanced on it.

When it is time for you to shine, all you need do is bend the straw about a third of the way from the bottom. Poke the doubled end through the neck of the bottle. Once the bent part is inside the bottle it will try to unfold.

At this point, it looks something like this.

Tip the straw so that the bent corner is pressed against one side of the bottle. Push the corner down so the end inside the bottle touches the side of the bottle opposite the one the bent corner touches. The tip *must* touch the other side and be pointing slightly upward.

Lift carefully, and up comes the bottle. You

can even raise a bottle which is partly full of water, if you choose your bottle correctly.

Experiment first. Otherwise, you may become your own victim.

The Coin Under the Cup

Some tricks work most of the time. This excellent trick *almost always* works. Once in a while, though, a victim may turn the tables and outsmart you.

You need two coins that are alike: two pennies or two quarters or whatever. Place one coin on a table. Keep the other in your pocket.

Hand your victim a cup that you can't see through, like one made from Styrofoam. Say, "Please put the cup upside down over the coin."

When this is done, ask whether the victim is certain the coin is still under the cup.

Of course he or she is certain.

"Just to make sure do you want to check?" you ask.

It does not matter whether the victim checks or not. The important part is to get your victim used to picking up the cup.

When the victim peeks and says the coin is still under the cup, it's time for some stagecraft.

"I can remove that coin without moving the cup," you announce grandly.

Ask the victim or someone else to put a bowl or a pan over the cup.

Then have someone put a towel over the bowl or pan. This stacking of items can go on as long as you want to keep putting things over the coin.

Eventually, it is time to perform. Make a few "magic" motions over the pile of coverings. You can mutter a few "magic" words.

Then remove the top item from the pile. Make another motion. Utter a few words. Take away the next covering.

Play out this performance with style. Finally, you will get down to the cup. At this point, tap the bottom of the cup with your index finger. This keeps everyone looking at the cup.

Take the second coin from your pocket without letting anyone know what you are doing. Keep it hidden in your hand.

After tapping the cup a few times, step

back. Hold both hands together over your head.

"Without moving the cup, I have succeeded."

When asked to prove this, you show the coin you took from your pocket. Most victims will immediately lift the cup to check on the original coin.

When that happens, quickly grab the coin from under the cup.

Give everyone your best smile. "See? I took the coin from under the cup but I did not have to remove the cup."

Sure, this is a dirty trick. But being a trickster can be a dirty job.

The Stubborn Card

Many people take it personally when they cannot do something. When this happens, they try harder and harder to do it. Maybe they have to prove that they are stronger or smarter than the trick that fooled them.

Here is just the trick for the person who can't stand being outdone—because it can't be done, however easy it seems.

A piece of file card—about two inches long by three inches wide—is great for this trick. Any piece of stiff paper will work, however. Cut it to approximately that size.

Bend down each of the long sides about one-quarter of an inch. When you're finished, the card should look like this:

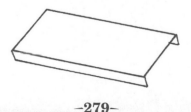

Set the card on a table or desk. (The slicker the surface, the better.)

"Just blow hard under that card, hard enough to turn it over," you command. Then stand back and watch frustration set in.

The card slips and skids around, but is practically impossible to blow over.

Some people make it turn over when they blow down on the table several inches *in front* of the card. They can't make the card turn over no matter where they blow.

Do set one ground rule to begin with: "If you blow the card off the table, you lose." This keeps you from ending up on the wrong end of a good trick.

Paper Strong Man

Fold a paper napkin in half lengthwise, then roll it tightly into a tube the size of a thick pencil. Next, twist the roll to make it even tighter. Hand it to someone and instruct that person to grasp the napkin so that one end is held in each hand. Then challenge the person to pull straight apart and tear the napkin into two pieces.

This sounds easy. It isn't. Very few people can actually pull the napkin apart in this manner. Make sure everyone realizes it is fair to pull only in a straight line. It is not fair to put the twisted napkin over the corner of a table or on any other sharp surface.

After everyone is satisfied that this is a pretty difficult feat of strength, it is time for you to make your bet.

"I bet I can do it." That should be enough to rile others who have been unsuccessful.

They'll claim you can't but it's easy once you know how. Just wet the paper napkin in the middle. Wait a second or two, then pull. The water weakens the paper and makes it easy to pull apart. Bet you didn't know your own strength!

Trapped by a Bottleneck

Place a soda bottle upside down on a dollar bill as shown below. As you can see, the bottle has the dollar trapped under it. The challenge is to remove the dollar bill from under the bottle without tipping the bottle over.

Don't touch the bottle. Don't pick it up. Don't hold it steady. Don't brace anything against the bottle to steady it. Just remove the dollar without tipping, moving, or touching the bottle.

If this one stumps you, check the upside-down

answer. But don't give up too soon. It is a lot easier than it looks at first glance.

Turn the page upside down for the answer.

All you need do to meet the dare is roll one end of the dollar bill tightly around a pencil. Keep rolling the pencil toward the bottle. The bill will slowly slide out from under the bottle, leaving the bottle standing on end.

Don't Fold Up

When you say, "I bet you can't fold a piece of paper in half ten times," you're almost sure to get an answer to your dare.

The rules are simple: Your opponent picks any piece of paper he or she wishes. It may be as large or as small, as thick or as thin as your victim wishes. The steps are just as easy to understand: Fold the paper in half; next, fold it in half again. Then again...and again...and again. Each time, make the paper half the size it was before the fold.

Folds may be horizontal or vertical, even diagonal if your opponent wishes. It really doesn't matter.

What does matter is that, no matter the size or thinness of the paper, no one—*but no one*—is ever going to be able to fold it the tenth time. Paper is simply mightier than human muscles.

Try it yourself. Just to be sure.

That Tears It

While your victim watches you closely, make two same-sized tears in a piece of paper. That leaves the paper looking something like this fat letter M.

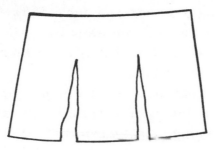

Give your victim your best smile and say, "I bet you can't hold one end of the paper in each hand and tear off both ends in one quick pull."

Your victim will probably study the tears and, since they are the same length, take you up on it.

You'll win every time. Only one end will tear free every time. You can bet on it.

Blow by Blow

Put a ping-pong ball on a table. Blow steadily on it and watch it roll away from you. When everyone is convinced it is an ordinary ball, you can make your move.

Put the ball in a kitchen funnel. (Hold the funnel so the wide mouth is up, and the small opening points down.)

Tell your listeners, "I bet that, blowing steadily, no one here can blow this ball up and out of this funnel."

Naturally, such an easy task gets lots of takers. It also causes lots of frustration. No matter how hard a person blows steadily upward through the funnel, the ball will not fly out of the funnel. It spins and turns and

even hops around a bit, but it stays in the funnel through even the windiest of blows.

The trick? Don't let players blow in short spurts. Make it clear they may blow as hard and as long as they wish, but they must blow a steady stream of air into the funnel.

It seems so easy but that ball is there to stay.

For Windy Characters

Blow up a balloon so that others watch you do it. Then let the air out. Push the deflated balloon's fat end into the mouth of a soda bottle. Stretch the balloon's narrow opening over the mouth of the bottle. Let everyone see exactly what you are doing.

Tell the others, "I bet no one can blow up the balloon so that it fills the bottle."

Since everyone just saw you blow up the balloon, and the bottle is so small, it looks like an easy bet to win. It is. For you.

Others may huff and puff but they simply

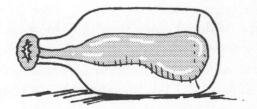

can't blow up the balloon to the point it fills the inside of the bottle. With every bit the balloon expands, it gets harder and harder to blow up.

There is no trick to it. Your victims can't blow up the balloon in the bottle. Neither could you if you tried. It's a matter of air pressure, which makes this balloon in the bottle a match for any windbag.

It's a Toss-up

Remove a paper match from a matchbook with an adult's permission. Carefully tear the head from the match and dispose of the flammable head safely. Show the paper part to your audience.

Tell your victim, "I bet I can make this match land on its edge on the table every time I toss it in the air. If it lands on either flat side you win. If it lands on either edge I win."

Most people will accept your bet. If your opponent wants to check the match by tossing it a few times, that's fine. However, once the bet is made you must be the one to toss the match into the air.

Can you figure out how to make sure you win each and every time? Bend the match in half just before you throw it in the air. This will guarantee it lands on its edge. Will your friend laugh or cry foul? It's a toss-up.

Stand Firm

People admire those who take a firm stand. With this stunt you can take a firm stand yourself.

Drop a sheet of paper on the floor and announce, "I can stand on this paper in such a way that nobody can push me off."

Naturally a dare like that won't go unanswered. When someone accepts it, be sure everyone understands the rules.

Tell the group you must be allowed to place the paper in a location of your own choice. Only one opponent may challenge you at a time. Each of you will stand with at least one foot on the paper. Your opponent may touch only you in trying to push you from the paper, not another object that in turn touches or pushes you from the paper. In order to win, all you have to do is stand firm and not be pushed or pulled off the paper.

After you agree on the rules, you are on your way to winning. Place the paper in the middle of a doorway and be ready to stand on the side where the door opens into the room. Position your opponent to stand on the paper on the other side of the doorway.

Close the door between you.

When you stand on the part of the paper that extends into the room beneath the closed door there isn't a way in the world your opponent can push or pull you from the paper!

The Doors Are Open

On this page you see the floor plan of a strange building. Imagine that the building is a prison built by a judge with a very odd sense of humor.

As you can see, there is an open door in each wall of each room. (Some rooms actually have two doors in one wall due to the crazy way the prison is built.)

The judge offered his prisoners freedom if they could do one thing. The one thing was easy enough. All any prisoner had to do was

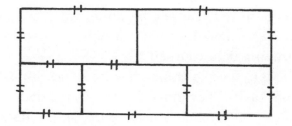

to start somewhere either inside or outside the prison building. From that starting point, the prisoner merely had to go through each door in the prison one time—and one time only. Any prisoner who did this was too smart to be in prison, the judge said, and would be released immediately.

By now you are saying you could have gotten out. You couldn't. The judge knew this task was impossible. It can't be done. As we said, the judge had a strange sense of humor. Since no prisoner ever completed the task, he never had to let anyone out of prison.

Even so, you will want to try. Start at any point. Go through each door one time and once only. It cannot be done. Like the prisoners, though, you'll probably insist on proving it to yourself.

Many people think they have accomplished the task. They haven't. In every case they either go through a door twice, skip a door, or go through the wall. Or, in drawing the prison, they forget to put in one door or put in one extra. Watch for these mistakes as you bet someone they can't get out of prison even when all the doors are left wide open.

Draw the Answer

Here's the problem. Look closely at the drawing below for ten seconds or so.

Now, take a pencil in hand and copy the figure below onto another sheet of paper.

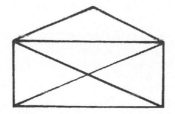

Start at any point on the drawing you wish. Draw the figure as it is shown on page 295, without ever lifting your pencil from the paper or going over any lines you have already drawn.

Not very many people do it correctly in one try. Are you one of them?

If you goof up the first time, don't peek at the answer. Try it again and again until you solve the puzzle.

Though almost everyone can do this puzzle, it is a fairly safe bet that most people won't finish it correctly on their first try.

Answer at top of next page.

Turn the page upside down for the answer.

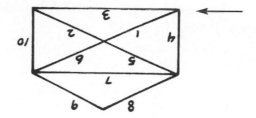

Invert and Escape

Arrange four pencils and an eraser on a table so they form the outline of a football passing through a goalpost, as shown on the following page. Toothpicks also work instead of pencils.

Make your bet when you say that by moving just two of the pencils you will not only turn the outline of the goal upside down, you'll make the eraser miss the goal at the same time. Promise that when you turn the goal over, it will have the same shape it now has.

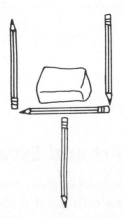

Let your opponents try this on their own a time or two to decide whether they will take your bet or not. For that matter, try it by yourself now. Can you win your own bet?

Check the answer when you either think you have solved the problem or when you have given up. It is really very easy.

Turn the page upside down for the answer.

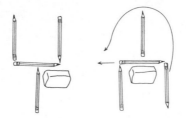

Move the two pencils as shown by the arrows.

THAT'S A NASTY TRICK

Underwater Challenge

A good way to start this prank is to fill a tall glass with water. Then, when everyone is watching, drop a coin into the water.

After the coin has settled to the bottom of the glass, you state your challenge:

"I am going to set this glass on the table. If you can get the coin out without spilling any of the water in the glass, the coin is yours."

There has to be a way to do this. You can expect a poor pigeon to volunteer.

"There is just one catch," you continue. "I

want your word that once you begin you won't quit. No one likes a quitter!"

So who is going to quit without getting that coin? By now your victim is all but diving into the glass for the coin.

"One last warning. I am going to set the glass on the table myself. Are you still sure you want to do this? I would hate to be responsible for turning you into a quitter."

By now, you have made such a thing about of being a quitter there is not a way in the world your victim will back down. Therefore, it is once again sly time.

You need a piece of fairly stiff paper. File folder paper works just fine. A piece about four by five inches or so is great.

Cover the open mouth of the glass with the paper. Hold the paper firmly in place with your palm. Invert the glass so that the open end of the glass, covered by the paper, is facing down.

Give the water just a second or two to wet the paper. Now, being as careful as you have ever been, it is time to remove your hand.

Without moving the paper even a fraction of an inch, hold the glass just above the tabletop. As you lower the glass onto the table, let go of the paper. If it's wet enough, it will stay stuck in place as you ease the glass onto the table. Not one drop of water will leak out, if you do this carefully.

Now what you have looks like this.

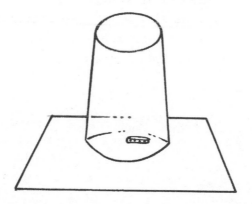

(By the way, don't set this up on top of a tablecloth or place mat. If you do, the cloth will become a wet sponge and your victim will die laughing as you clean up the mess.)

Now comes the tricky part. Slowly and with care, you must slip the paper out from under the glass of water. Hold the glass pressed down with one hand and pull out the paper with the other. If you lose a few drops of water just clean them up with a cloth.

Then, with a wave of your hand, present the glass and coin to your victim.

"Give it your best shot," you may wish to say. "Just remember the rules. Don't spill any water. And don't give up."

Give It Up

This stunt has been frustrating victims for years. It's a play on words, which begins with the victim expecting some sort of magic trick. It usually ends with the victim having a few words for you!

Tell someone you have a very special coin trick. To demonstrate this trick you need two coins of the *same* denomination: two dimes or two quarters or two whatever. Once the victim hands you the two coins you are ready to begin.

"Look closely at these two coins," you command.

The victim does so, naturally.

"You are going to have to identify these coins again in just a second or two. You may even want to check the dates and mint marks," you say.

After your victim is positive he or she can

identify the coins, you place them in one of your hands. Put that hand behind your back along with your other hand. Pass the coins back and forth once or twice. If you want to create suspense you can do this for quite some time. You may even wish to mumble some magic words.

Eventually, hold one coin in each hand. Bring both hands out in front of you. Hold them, palms up, and open them.

"Now," you tell your victim, "tell me which of these two coins you just gave me."

Certainly, you were given both the coins. Your victim knows this and so do you.

"I gave you both of them!" is the natural reaction.

It is your turn to look puzzled. "Are you certain? Look carefully at them. Are you positive you gave me both of these coins?"

"Yes. Of course I'm certain." This or something close to it is what you can expect as an answer.

"If you are sure you gave me both of these coins, why thanks. I appreciate the gift!" Smile—and put the coins in your pocket. Watch your victim's face as he or she realizes your play on words is the only trick involved.

Whether you actually keep the coins your victim "gave" to you is another question. If you do, you may lose a friend. You may get punched in the nose. Or your victim may have a good laugh and go looking another pigeon to play the trick on.

Tricky Trap

Some people just seem to beg to be put down. You know the ones. They boast and brag and act as if they know more than anyone else.

Tricky Trap is designed for just this sort of character. It works best when a few other people are around to see you put one over on the loudmouth.

Fill two glasses a little more than half full of water. (If you want to be on the safe side, use unbreakable glasses.) Make a real drama out of filling and checking the water level in the glasses. The amount of water really doesn't matter, but when you pretend it does, you build the interest of your audience.

Once you're satisfied with the amount of water in the glasses, it's time to set up your victim.

"This trick needs steady hands and real concentration," you may begin. "Not everyone is up to it. In fact, I don't want any people to volunteer to try it unless they're absolutely sure they're going to be able to hold these glasses without spilling the water in them."

What big shot can turn down a challenge like that? When your victim assures you he or she is the one for the job, you're on the way.

"Hold out both hands, palms down," you command.

Carefully, place one glass on the back of each hand.

"Can you handle these by yourself?" Act as if you're afraid your victim lacks the strength to hold the glasses.

"Are you positive you can do this without spilling even a drop?"

Your victim is certain, naturally. This is a snap.

"Great!" Smile at your victim and walk away.

It may take a minute or so for the realization to sink in, but your victim is in the Tricky Trap. How does someone go about getting two glasses of water off the backs of both hands without spilling a drop? It doesn't help when everyone in the room is laughing at the poor sap.

What happens next is pretty much up to

you. You may want to take this loudmouth off the hook and remove the glasses yourself. Or not.

What's It Worth?

This nasty little trick is really a play on words and a great put-down.

Pretend you're trying to tear a sheet of notebook paper into four equal pieces. (You can turn this into a real production, if you want.) Fold the paper into fourths. Then crease each fold. Work at making the paper tear along each crease. Yet no matter how hard you try, one of the tears always leaves the crease.

Fooling around with the paper, you may make this a quick stunt or drag it out for several minutes. At any rate, your victim will eventually get into the act, and then it's easy for you to set it up.

Pretend to be indignant and upset. "So you think it is easy to tear a paper into fourths. Well, it isn't."

Your victim will probably insist there's nothing to it.

"I'll tell you what," you can exclaim. "If you can tear a sheet of paper into four pieces the same size, I'll give you a quarter. But I don't think you can do it."

Now there's a challenge no one can turn down. When your victim hands you the required pieces of paper, be sure to say what a fine job of tearing it was.

"You tore the paper into exact quarters," you can say. Hand one of the pieces to your victim. "Here is the quarter I promised you."

Of course, a quarter of the paper was not what was expected. It is also true that you have kept your tricky word.

Three Can't Be Four

Are you the sort of trick-player who won't stop at anything? Are you the type of person who never gets bothered by how sneaky a trick may be? Do you enjoy really irritating your friends? If so, this trick is for you!

Hold three quarters in one hand. Look at them and remark, "These four quarters are all just a little different, aren't they?" Hold

the three quarters toward your victim.

Naturally, your victim will say something such as "There are only three quarters in your hand."

Pretend to be surprised. Hold up the quarters and study them with care. "Are you sure? Did you say three? I see four."

Since you probably have a reputation as a trickster by now, your victim knows something is coming. Even so, who could resist insisting that there are only three quarters in your hand?

Ruttle the quarters around in your closed fist and check again. "I see four."

By now, it has become something of a crusade for your victim. There are only three quarters in your hand. Your friend is absolutely certain about that.

How long you wish to continue the debate is up to you. It also depends on how long your victim will put up with such nonsense.

You can decide when the time has come to spring the trap using this dare:

"I still see four quarters in my hand. You think there are only three. Look, if you're so positive, will you give me another quarter if I'm wrong?"

By now, your victim is ready to do battle. If you have set the stage properly, and if your victim reacts as most people do, the answer will come quickly.

"Yes—sure."

At this point most people don't really listen to what you say. They're too intent on the quarters in your hand.

"Well, I am wrong. You are right. There are only three quarters in my hand. Since I am wrong, you owe me the quarter you just promised."

You may need to review what you said about getting another quarter if you are wrong. Even then you probably won't collect the quarter. But no matter whether you get the money or not, you have added one more success to your score.

The Severed Finger

This trick is what people sometimes call a "heart-stopper." That's because victims are so surprised, they may think their hearts either have stopped or leaped right up into their throats.

To make The Severed Finger work, you have to do some careful preparation. The first step is to find a small cardboard box that's about four inches wide, six inches long and an inch or so deep. Don't worry about finding one exactly that size—just come close.

Cut a hole in the bottom of the box as shown in the drawing. This hole should be

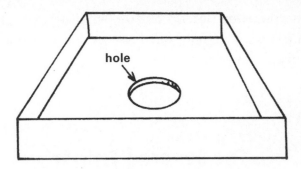

hole

just big enough so that your index or middle finger will fit through it.

Now add some makeup to your finger to give it a really repulsive look. A little bit of rouge caked below the bottom knuckle will make the finger look as though traces of blood are sticking to it. Some pale face powder or blush rubbed into the finger gives it a dead look.

Poke your made-up finger through the hole in the box. Arrange white cloth or cotton

matting in the bottom so that it looks as if your finger is lying in a nest of cloth inside the box. Cover the entire bottom of the box carefully, so there's no sign of the hole.

Put the lid back on the box and hold it with your other hand under it as well. This keeps your victims from realizing your finger is poked through the bottom.

To make this trick work, you have to give it a good buildup. Be sure to look solemn and serious. You can begin like this:

"There was a terrible car accident in front of our house last night. Three people had to be taken to the hospital."

Now that you have the victim's attention you can really develop your story.

"One of the children got her finger cut off. There was a lot of blood and she cried and cried."

Pause just a second or two to let your words sink in.

"After everyone was gone I found her finger. It was lying in the grass. Since I didn't know what to do with it I put it in the freezer last night. I have it here in this box. What do you think I should do with it?"

Pull the top off the box. There is a human finger lying all bloody and pale in the bottom of the box.

Let your victim stare at the finger for a few seconds. Usually people are so curious they bend forward to see better. Then wiggle the finger in the box.

After your victim yells or screams or faints you can show off how the trick works. Then both of you can go in search of someone else to trick with this gruesome stunt.

QUICK TRICKS

Never Seen Before
and Never Seen Again

This trick has been around for hundreds of years. It probably first began as a riddle. Then someone turned the riddle into a trick.

Tell someone, "In just a minute I'll show you something no one living has ever seen before. After I have shown it to you no one will ever see it again."

This sounds pretty spooky. Naturally, your victim has to be interested.

Crack the shell of a nut of any kind. A

peanut is great since you can crack its thin shell in your fingers.

Hold up the nut inside. "See this. No one has ever seen it before."

Then quickly eat the nut. Once you have swallowed it, wind up the trick:

"And now, no one will ever see it again."

Never mind the groans. You told the truth!

There's a Trick to It

Are you game for what seems an impossible problem, which has an obvious answer? If so, this one is for you. Just look closely for the tricky phrase that makes it all possible.

Place a quarter on a table. Place a penny beside it. The object of the stunt is to move the penny *under* the quarter. You may touch the penny. You may not touch the quarter in any way, shape, or form. Do not use anything, not even a piece of paper, to move the quarter. It must be left exactly as it is.

When you figure this one out, read on to check you answer. Then go looking for someone to be your dupe.

Got it yet? All you have to do is pick up the penny and hold it under the table beneath the spot where the quarter rests. The penny is now under the quarter, just as promised.

There is an even sneakier variation of this stunt. After putting one coin on top of the table, you say, "It's easy to place this second coin under the one on the table. You may not touch the coin on the table. *But* you may hit the table on its top or its side, if you want."

Just be sure you're using a strong, heavy table. It's fun to watch your victims try to get the coin to bounce high enough for them to slide the other coin under it. Of course, it won't work!

When in Rome . . .

One of the best things the Romans did for us was to give us Roman numerals. Their system of writing numerals helps you invent some great tricks!

Here's an example. Translate this equation into Roman numerals on a piece of paper: 11 + 1 = 10. Write it really large—even though it's wrong. It should be easy to read.

$$XI + I = X$$

Be sure your victim knows the equation is *wrong*. You may even want to mutter, "Eleven plus one does *not* equal ten. But I know this equation is correct."

If your friend happens to spot the error

before you make that comment, you may say, "It just looks wrong. I know it's right."

As soon as your friendly opponent insists the equation is wrong, it's time to make your pitch.

"I can correct it. I won't touch the paper. I won't erase anything on the paper. No one will have to change the paper in any way. Yet the equation will be correct."

This seems impossible. Most people will suggest you have just misplaced your mind.

When you are ready to show your stuff, casually walk to the other side of the table. Look! You now see the original equation upside down. It looks like this: X = I + IX (ten equals one plus nine).

It *is* correct. How about that?

Three into Four

This quick brain buster is a good trick. You can do it without any preparation. If your victims catch on, congratulate them. If no one sees through the trick, your reputation as a tricky person blossoms.

Place three toothpicks or drinking straws on a tabletop.

"Can you make these three things into four?" you ask. "You may not bend or break or cut or damage any of the three."

If you're really sure of yourself and want to get someone's goat you might add, "The average second-grader does this in 32 seconds." Then start counting seconds.

If your victim fails, everyone laughs at a person who could not beat a second-grader. If he or she is successful, so what? Anybody should be able to do better than a second-grader.

Here's the simple solution in Roman or Arabic numerals. Making three objects into four is a snap—either way.

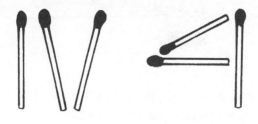

Four for Sure

See whether you can figure out how to win each of the following bets. After you've seen through each, or given up and checked the answer, you're ready to add five more sure-fire "gotchas" to your collection of ways to triumph over friends and foes alike.

Bet one. Tell your opponent, "I bet I can write a longer word than you."

Most people will search their minds or even the dictionary for long words. No matter what they write, you will win your bet. Reread the bet carefully to guess how this can be so.

Bet two. For this one, you need a deck of cards. Hand the deck to your victim. Tell this lucky person, "I bet I can hand you any card from the deck that you select, even after you hide it back in the deck. You may

shuffle the deck as many times as you wish. All I ask is that you keep thinking of the card you have chosen."

No matter how carefully your victim shuffles the deck, you will always be able to hand back the proper card. Do you see how to win this bet?

Bet three. Here's a bet with a solution so simple it is almost impossible to figure out for most people. Just tell someone, "I bet I can drop a spoonful of sugar (or a lump of

sugar) into a cup of coffee without getting the sugar wet."

No, you don't wrap the sugar in plastic! Can you see through this bet?

Bet four. Have someone write six or eight words on a piece of paper. Make sure it's done in a way that doesn't allow you to see what is written on the paper. Then ask the person to fold the paper two or three times so the words are completely hidden from

view. Last, but certainly most important, have your victim place the paper on the floor and cover it with one foot.

Now say, "In spite of all the precautions you have taken, I bet I can tell you what is on that paper." And of course you can! Every time you find a victim, you'll win this bet.

Answers on page 332.

Turn the page upside down for the answers.

One. Write "a longer word than you."

Two. Hand your victim the entire deck of cards. You've handed back the chosen card.

Three. Drop the sugar into a cup of dry coffee grounds.

Four. Tell your victim that there is a foot on the paper. Because there is.

Paper Puff

Tear paper so you have three or four pieces about the size of postage stamps. Place them on the back of your hand.

Tell your victims, "In one big puff, I'm going to blow *all but one* of these papers off my hand. Just to make it harder, I want you to choose the one piece of paper that I won't blow off."

Encourage them to pick the papers up and look at them carefully. Let them rearrange the papers on your hand. The one rule is that the papers may not touch each other. (This means that they may not be stacked on top of each other either.)

When the one paper is selected, it's time for you to prove you can do what you claim—and you can!

Here's the trick. Press a finger of your free hand firmly on the paper that is to remain in place. Then blow.

The other pieces of paper flutter away and the chosen one remains, *exactly* as you said.

Remember to pick up the fallen paper. People may forgive you for tricking them, but nobody likes a litterbug.

Where's the Water?

Set up this trick by pulling a facial tissue out of its box. Pretend to examine it very carefully.

"These tissues are really strong," you can say to begin. "I think this tissue is much stronger than it looks."

Show the tissue to your intended victim. "Can you see how close together those fibers are."

Then, as though the thought just struck, you add, "I think you could carry more than a tablespoon of water in this tissue without crumpling it up or resting it on your hand. Don't you think so?"

Of course, your victim doesn't think so. How ridiculous even to consider carrying water in a facial tissue!

If your victim says it's impossible, offer to prove that it can be done. Should your victim think it is possible, ask to see how.

Either way, you've got your trick going.

Head straight for the nearest kitchen. When a person pours or runs water into the facial tissue the result is a soggy mess. So what else is new?

To prove your point, make your victim hold the tissue flat, using both hands. Open the freezer door and take out an ice cube. Place the cube on the tissue and instruct your pigeon to carry it across the room. It's as simple as that.

If your victim protests, ask, "Well, what is ice?"

The only possible answer is "frozen water."

If that's not good enough, hand the ice cube to your friend.

"Hold onto this for a few minutes. When it starts to melt you'll have all the water you want."

That should be all it takes. You've won again.

Now You See It—Now You Don't

Even when they know they are being set up for a trick, most people can't resist falling for it.

When you hold up a card or a bracelet or any small object and pretend to study it, people wonder what you are up to.

"You know, I can make this become invisible," you say. Turn the object and look at it from another angle. "Actually, I can make this item invisible to you but not to the others in the room." You look directly at your newest victim when you speak.

This can't be so. "No way," your victim will say to you. Then he or she will probably add, "You're trying to trick me, aren't you?"

Just smile and shrug. "There's only one way to find out."

Someone will ask that you demonstrate.

"Here is how it works," you can tell them. "I will make this object invisible to one person but not to the rest of us and it'll only take a second." Stand in front of your victim and add, "I'll stand right here in front of you so we're both watching it, but it doesn't matter where anybody else stands."

The catch is disgustingly simple. Quickly put the object on top of the victim's head. Expect others to moan and groan. It does not matter. You've done what you said you'd do.

Just don't play this trick in a room where the victim can look into a mirror.

Easy Under

Place one coin on top of a desk or table. Hand a second coin to the person you've chosen to be your victim.

"It's easy to place this coin under the one on the table," you tell your victim. "I can do it without moving the coin on the table or even touching it."

It won't take most victims long before they are willing to admit defeat.

Take the coin in one hand and hold it under the table or desk.

"Now it is under the coin on the table," you can tell them. Of course, the victim already sees that he or she has been duped. Explaining your success may not be necessary.

There is an even sneakier variation of this stunt. After putting one coin on top of the table, you say, "It's easy to place this second coin under the one on the table. You may not touch the coin on the table. But you may hit the table on its top or its side if you want."

Just be sure you're using a strong, heavy table. It's fun to watch your victims try to get the coin to bounce high enough for them to slide the other coin under. Of course, it won't work!

Two Cookies, Two Caps, One Trick

"I have magic powers," is one way to introduce this stunt. "I can put two things under two baseball caps. Then I can eat the two things. Afterward, I can put them back under *one* of the two caps."

Expect some rude guesses about your

methods when you make this claim. You may pretend to be offended and respond by gagging and saying, "That's gross! No way!"

When you're told to put up or shut up, the trick is easy. Place one cookie or one cracker under each of two caps.

"I have now put two things under two caps," you may explain. (This way, even the slowest member of the group stays with the stunt.)

Remove the caps and eat the cookies. You may even say something such as "Um. Good."

It is not necessary, but you can now explain,

"See, I have eaten the two things."

Finally, put on one of the caps. Smile—and wait for applause.

Do you have to tell your victims you have now put the two things under one of the caps? Surely, they aren't that slow...or are they?

A Quick Conclusion

What better way to end this book than with a trio of quick bets that are unbelievably easy but quite often catch others off guard. Here's a hint, though. Use only one of these per person.

Quick bet one. "I'll bet I can tell you a word almost everyone pronounces incorrectly."

Quick bet two. "I bet I know a word

which little children and adults all say wrong every time they use it."

Quick bet three. "I bet I know of a word that you and I always pronounce correctly each time we speak it."

Maybe you're a sharp enough trickster by now to see through these. If you need to check yourself, just read the upside-down answers.

Turn the page upside down for the answer.

One. Incorrectly
Two. Wrong
Three. Correctly

Index

If you liked this book, you'll love all this series:

Little Giant® Book of "True" Ghost Stories • Little Giant® Book of "True" Ghostly Tales • Little Giant® Book of After School Fun • Little Giant® Book of Amazing Mazes • Little Giant® Book of Animal Facts • Little Giant® Book of Basketball • Little Giant® Book of Brain Twisters • Little Giant® Book of Card Games • Little Giant® Book of Card Tricks • Little Giant® Book of Cool Optical Illusions • Little Giant® Book of Dinosaurs • Little Giant® Book of Dominoes • Little Giant® Book of Eerie Thrills & Unspeakable Chills • Little Giant® Book of Giggles • Little Giant® Book of Insults & Putdowns • Little Giant® Book of Jokes • Little Giant® Book of Kids' Games • Little Giant® Book of Knock-Knocks • Little Giant® Book of Laughs • Little Giant® Book of Magic Tricks • Little Giant® Book of Math Puzzles • Little Giant® Book of Mini-Mysteries • Little Giant® Book of Optical Illusion Fun • Little Giant® Book of Optical Illusions • Little Giant® Book of Optical Tricks • Little Giant® Book of Riddles • Little Giant® Book of School Jokes • Little Giant® Book of Science Experiments • Little Giant® Book of Science Facts • Little Giant® Book of Side-Splitters • Little Giant® Book of Tongue Twisters • Little Giant® Book of Travel Fun • Little Giant® Book of Travel Games • Little Giant® Book of Tricks & Pranks • Little Giant® Book of Visual Tricks • Little Giant® Book of Weird & Wacky Facts • Little Giant® Book of Whodunits

Available at fine stores everywhere.